An Educatio

An Education for Rita

A Memoir, 1975–1985

Brinda Karat

Best wishes,
Brinda Karat

LeftWord

First published in January 2024.
Reprinted January 2024.

LeftWord Books
2254/2A, Shadi Khampur
New Ranjit Nagar
New Delhi 110008
INDIA

LeftWord Books and Vaam Prakashan are imprints of
Naya Rasta Publishers Pvt. Ltd.

leftword.com

ISBN   978-93-92018-21-3 (paperback)
        978-93-92018-22-0 (e-book)

Printed and bound by Chaman Enterprises, New Delhi.

For
my comrades in the
Kapda Mazdoor Lal Jhanda Union
and
in memory of
Ashoka and Kalindi

Contents

IV. HERE COME THE WOMEN

V. A DECADE CLOSES

CONTENTS

'Comrade Rita'

I remember that night as though it were yesterday. We were in a small office in Kamla Nagar, a locality in north Delhi, not far from the Birla Cotton Textile Mill. There were about fourteen of us — apart from me, all were workers from the mill. The meeting had to be held at night, since that week many of the workers were in the middle shift, which finished at 9.30 pm. The main door was shut tight, the only light was from a flickering oil lamp in the middle of the room. We were sitting on the floor, as there was not enough space for so many chairs. It was my first meeting with the Birla Mills branch — a meeting of members of the Communist Party of India (Marxist) (CPI(M)) who worked in the mill. I had waited years for this day.

It was August 1975, two months after Indira Gandhi had declared the Emergency. The period of the Emergency in India is generally viewed as one of destruction of civil liberties and democratic rights, which, of course, it was. What is sometimes given less attention is that the Emergency was also a concerted and targeted assault on the working classes and led to a dismantling of the regulations, which were seen as fetters to the development of aggressive capitalism.

The Emergency came as a boon to India's capitalists. The leading business houses in India had been shaken by the sweep of working-class struggles and militancy in the early seventies. The historic railway worker's strike of 1974 led to a series of solidarity actions. The Emergency eliminated the basic right to unionise, to protest, to strike. It thus disarmed the working classes of their hard-won rights and gave a free hand to capitalists who sought to 'discipline' workers. In an interview with the *New York Times*,

India's leading industrialist of the time, J.R.D. Tata put it plainly. 'Things have gone too far', he said. 'You can't imagine what we have gone through here — strikes, boycotts, demonstrations. Why, there were days I couldn't walk out of my office into the street. The parliamentary system is not suited to our needs.' Many of India's trade union leaders had been arrested.

In our meeting that night, the workers were discussing how the Emergency had emboldened the management to impose greater workloads on the workers and how we could organise resistance to this. Leading the discussion was Comrade Sriram, a former worker dismissed for his union work, who was now a respected leader. Sriram's appearance belied his strength. He was thin, with hunched shoulders, probably a result of excessive bidi smoking, which had resulted in a weak chest. He suddenly turned to me and said, 'I have received information that your room in Calcutta has been broken into and searched. Comrade Surjeet has sent this message, so we must take it seriously. You have been told to work here under a new name'. Comrade Sriram was referring to Harkishan Singh Surjeet, a member of the Polit Bureau of the CPI(M).

I was not surprised. My rented rooms in Calcutta were used for a few days by some of our leaders who had to go underground the week following the Emergency. The police had probably got wind of it, although months later! I suggested I could be called Sheila. There was a chorus of 'No' to the name. It turned out that Sriram's wife's name was Sheila, and it would cause confusion to have two Sheilas. Chandrabhan, a worker in the spinning department and former wrestler from western Uttar Pradesh could never pronounce my name, Brinda. He always called me Birinder. My repeated efforts to correct his pronunciation had come to nought. It was probably with relief that he enthusiastically welcomed the suggestion to rename me. He said, 'Let's have a name that is easy to pronounce. We will call you Rita'.

From that day, for the next ten years, I was known as Comrade Rita.

I

RETURN

London to Calcutta

I had given up my job in Air India's London office in 1970 and returned to my birthplace, Calcutta. My three years in London had upturned my life. I was a nineteen-year-old with dreams of joining drama school in London, driven by my passion for theatre. My father, who had a strong work ethic and believed that his daughters should be economically independent, suggested I get a job in London and join evening classes at a drama school. Helped by him, I first joined Air India in Calcutta for a few months and then applied for a vacancy in London. In 1967, I was posted to Heathrow airport.

I soon had a run-in with the management. There was an odd rule that women working at the airport could not wear the signature Air India saree uniform but had to compulsorily wear a skirt and jacket. My objections that an Indian airline should surely allow their staff to wear the national dress if she chose to were brushed aside. The English girls employed by Air India thought it was weird that when high fashion was a mini-skirt, I wanted to wear a saree. A situation was created when I continued to wear the uniform saree I had worn in Calcutta. My boss was a kind Scotsman named Alan who, instead of sacking me for insubordination, wrote to the Bombay head office for advice as to how to deal with this stubborn young woman. Within a few weeks came the answer from Bobby Kooka himself, the legendary commercial director of Air India who had been responsible, it was said, for the famous Maharaja logo. He wrote, 'Not only Brinda, but any other employee can choose to wear the saree'. I savoured the victory when my colleagues who had earlier made fun of my objections queued up in the restroom to learn how to wear a saree

Brinda, the drama school aspirant, in London.

from me! I applied to some of the drama schools and got admission to evening classes, which I could not attend because of my shift duties at the airport. But by the time I was transferred to the head office in Bond Street, the centre of London, it was mid-March of 1968, and my life was changing.

I had reconnected with my school friend Mala Sen, who later authored the bestselling book *Bandit Queen*, a sensitive rendering of the life of Phoolan Devi. She lived down the road from me with her partner, Farrukh Dhondy. He was a real live wire, brilliant, articulate, and a left-wing political activist at the time. Their small flat was always abuzz with young people in heated political discussions, all with strong opinions. I used to wait till my shift was done (I think only Mala and I were working among a group of students) and would bound up the narrow stairway to their flat at the very top of the building, where over cigarettes and numerous cups of tea, coffee, cheap red wine, young men and women would be discussing the fate of the world. It was my first introduction to left-wing political discussions. The London scene in the late sixties, somewhat similar to what was happening on US campuses and in colleges and universities in Europe, was of social churning, rebellions of young people against the status quo in all spheres. The slogan was — Question Everything. It was a potpourri of clashing views of the anarchists, the Trotskyists, the Black Power groups, the Marxists, the hippy movement, of poetry and songs calling for change, for revolution. The establishment was shaken. You could not be young in London in the late sixties and remain untouched.

What inspired me greatly was the national liberation struggle of Vietnam, this small nation fighting the might of the most powerful imperialist country in the world. I started participating in the processions and protests against the Vietnam war, taking off from work. I joined Mala and Farrukh's band of marchers at the famous Grosvenor Square protests in March and then the October march in 1968, which was baton-charged by mounted police. The Vietnam war made me want to study more of this ideology — Marxism — which had inspired the leaders of that small nation. I started reading Marxist literature, and that led me to learn about what was happening in India and my home state of West Bengal.

Most Indian students in England at the time were drawn to the Naxalite movement. One of the leading Indian student activists at the School of Oriental and African Studies (SOAS; now SOAS University of London) was Suneet Chopra. He considered himself a Marxist and was an old family friend from my school days in Calcutta. Suneet's younger sister Nina was close to my elder sister Junie, and his younger sister Madhu and I were roommates in college and were close friends. When we met in London, Suneet gifted me the book *To the Finland Station* by Edmund Wilson,

17

which traced the historical trajectory of progressive and socialist movements. Sunny, as he was affectionately called, was quite taken by the Naxalite movement in those days. One day, he brought a young Bengali student to my room, whom he insisted I was related to, and said here was a Naxalite who had escaped being imprisoned and that he could advise me. By that time, I was quite clear that my interest was to learn more about the CPI(M). Suneet was disappointed. He said to me, 'Binnie [my nickname], we will both go back to India, but alas, we will be on opposite sides of the barricade!' Several years later, when I visited the CPI(M) office in Delhi, I was delighted to see Suneet there. He said, 'Anyone who believes in Marxism and tries to apply it in India will know soon enough that it is this party which truly represents the cause of revolution'! I jokingly told him, 'Well that's a relief, I would have hated you to have been on the opposite side, taking pot shots at me'. Both sisters, Madhu and Nina, had joined the Left movement and were very much on the same side of the barricade, too. Later in this memoir, I refer to Nina Rao — none other than Sunny's sister. Sunny spent his political life in India building the Party among the rural poor and became a Central Committee member of the Party. Sadly, he died in April 2023 of a sudden heart attack. In those London days, it was so special to find that my childhood friends Mala, Suneet, Madhu, and Nina were all in the fight for a better world, inspired by socialism.

I had tried to get as much literature as I could lay my hands on about the Party and its outstanding and brilliant leaders. A.K. Gopalan, B.T. Ranadive, E.M.S. Namboodiripad, Jyoti Basu, and P. Sundarayya were some of the names I knew. But it was the developments in West Bengal that drew me to the CPI(M). We used to get Indian newspapers, including *The Statesman*, a Calcutta-based daily, in the Air India office, though a day late. I would scour the pages for news of the agitations sweeping West Bengal in the late sixties. Despite the strong anti-communist bias, the papers could not but report the massive scale of people's participation. I read about Jyoti Basu and his leadership both in the legislative assembly and outside in street protests. I was inspired by his fearlessness, speeches, and his role as a partisan in the struggle of workers and kisans. In West Bengal, the fight for food, land, and wages had faced strong repression. It was from mid-1968 to '69 that within me, too, there was a churning of my thoughts, my desires, my hopes. I started feeling caged by my job. I wanted to go back to India, to West Bengal, to join the Party.

It was about that time, during the autumn of 1969, that my close friend and later comrade, Subhashini Sahgal, who had been studying in the United States, was on her way home to India. We were the same age — twenty-two years old. We met excitedly at the Air India office. I said to her, 'I have something important to share with you', and she replied, 'Me too'. I can't remember now who said it first — 'I have become a communist'. We hugged each other tight, right there at the Air India reception. Subhashini returned to India and joined the Party, and for all these decades, we have stayed the closest of comrades and friends.

But I had to break the news to my father. I knew it was not going to be easy.

Family Ties

My father, Suraj Lal Dass, was born to a well-to-do Punjabi family living in Lahore. He was one of eight children. His father, Sukhdayal Dass, was, according to family lore, the first Indian in an important post in the Lahore postal services. Sukhdayal was known for being strongly anti-caste and gave up his caste name. He was progressive in his social approach, being a strong votary of widow remarriage and of women's education. His four daughters, my aunts, were all graduates, and the eldest was one of the first women doctors of her generation.

My grandmother Karam Kaur, born into a Sikh family, was sweet, gentle, and loving, caring for her large family of eight children. She had not studied beyond Class 3 and spoke only Punjabi. They lived in a large government bungalow in Lahore and lived a life of social, though not economic privilege. It was not a propertied family, and there was no inheritance for the children. In that sense, it could be said that in their professional lives, my father and his siblings were self-made. After he graduated from Government College, Lahore, my father came to Calcutta in the mid-1930s, having got a job with the Port Commissioner.

My grandparents and my younger aunts were forced to leave Lahore just before the terrible days of the Partition and came to India with little in their name, like hundreds of thousands of others. My father, many years later, joined a private company as an executive, finally becoming chairman of a British-owned company. Even though he was part of the corporate world — he was, in Calcutta's slang of the time, a Boxwala, as elite sections of corporate executives working for British companies were called — he had strong humanitarian values, a result, perhaps, of his own upbringing. We were brought up in a secular, liberal family environment, where conventions and social restrictions usually imposed on girls mattered little.

My mother was named Ashrukawna, or 'teardrop'. Some years before she was born, her parents had lost their first child. Her name, then, signified their sorrow and their longing for another child. Known as Kawna by her legions of friends and admirers, she had the reputation of being rebellious, talented, and always happy. She loved life.

My mother died in a car accident in 1952 when I was five years old. It was a tragedy that haunted us and influenced us four siblings through our growing-up years. Ma came from an illustrious Bengali family from both her paternal and maternal sides. Her mother, Mrinalini, described by an author of our family history as 'elegant and cultured', was the daughter of Hem Chandra Malik, an outspoken fighter for freedom against the British. Hem Chandra and his nephew Subodh Malik — later known as Raja Subodh Malik — were secret supporters of Anushilan Samiti, the militant nationalist group led by the legendary Aurobindo Ghose. Ma spent many days of her childhood in the joint Malik household, where her mother had been brought up in a world of anti-colonial commitment and intellectual discussion. I was told that Ma herself, as a young woman, was a follower of Subhas Chandra Bose. She, too, lost her mother when she was an adolescent. She was the only child, her elder sister having died tragically before Ma was born.

Ma's paternal grandfather, Ram Charan Mitra, had ten children, seven sons and three daughters. He was a government pleader in the Calcutta court and, after his retirement, became a legal advisor to big zamindari families. He had a string of properties and built seven adjoining houses for each of his sons, including my grandfather Phanindra Nath Mitra. This was in Jhamapukur, a locality in north Calcutta where my mother grew up. In contrast to the maternal side, the paternal side of my mother's family was conservative and orthodox.

Ashrukawna and Suraj, 1939.

The story goes that a young man, especially chosen for his impeccable Bengali 'bhadrolok' credentials by my grandfather as a potential husband for my mother, was to visit Jhamapukur to see her. As it happened, he had a close friend, a Punjabi whom he begged to accompany him. His friend tagged along reluctantly. Lahiri, the hopeful groom, lived to regret it! It was love at first sight — literally. The handsome Punjabi young man and the beautiful, vivacious Bengali girl fell in love. After several secret rendezvous, they declared their intention to get married. My grandfather was extremely unhappy. We found his diary many years later. It contained this terse note: 'Kawna has decided to marry the Punjabi'. It was unthinkable for him. He forbade anyone, including Ma's cousins in the joint family, to attend the wedding. But at least one cousin sister defied the ban and was at my mother's side at her wedding. It was the Malik side of her family who made all the arrangements. Ashrukawna and Suraj were married in a building which had historical significance: 12 Wellington Square, where the Maliks held meetings against the colonial plans to divide Bengal in 1905. When I think of my parents' wedding, I wonder if they ever discussed how lucky they were that their personal rebellion

22

was sanctified at a place with a history of resistance. The Malik family later donated this building to Calcutta University. It was only after his first grandchild was born that my grandfather made amends. He was a weekly visitor at his beloved daughter's home and would come laden with a huge container of delicious north Calcutta sweets for us grandchildren.

My parents got married in 1939 when marriages across caste and community were unusual. It was in such a household that we were brought up. After my mother's death, we were deprived of a strong, stable cultural anchor. Our knowledge of Bengali and Punjabi, let alone Hindi, was skin deep. We spoke mainly English at home. For several years, my aunts took turns to stay with us in Calcutta. When I think of those days, I marvel at their caring nature, leaving their own small children to come to Calcutta and look after us. My grandparents, too, were frequent visitors. We had a loving 'governess' — a term used during colonial times for a person who was a housekeeper, a teacher, and a carer of children, all rolled into one — called Humdum Baksh, who was an important figure in our childhood. A Muslim by birth who had converted to Christianity, she imposed a strict enough routine for us to be almost disciplined! So, it was an entirely eclectic upbringing. I had three siblings: my charismatic, large-hearted elder brother, Koko; my loving elder sister, Junie; and the youngest, Radhika, who, even then, was the wisest and kindest person you could meet. The deep bond between us four was the most powerful and enduring anchor in my life in those years after we lost our mother.

When my father received my letter conveying my intention to join the communists, he was horrified. He made a special trip to London. He felt it was fine to join protests but to give up my job to actually join the Party was something he found hard to accept. He tried to convince me, but I did not budge. He appealed to my siblings to intervene but found that both my sisters supported me while my elder brother remained neutral.

Thus it was that in early 1970, I returned to Calcutta.

23

Joining the Party

It was a struggle to get in touch with the Party. The CPI(M) was under severe attack — political, ideological, and physical, including the killing of communist cadres. It was considered extremely strange among Party circles that an upper-class girl with absolutely no political background should want to become a member. In bourgeois political parties, family connections open doors. I had the opposite experience. My class origin was the greatest disadvantage in my effort to join the CPI(M).

In those days in West Bengal, members of the Party were steeled in tremendous sacrifice and struggle. They had a high degree of ideological conviction, which gave them the courage to confront the daily risk of being attacked, even killed, by hired criminals of ruling class parties. While the Party faced repression and attacks in many states, the repression in West Bengal was particularly severe. The documents of the 1972 Madurai Congress of the Party record that 650 comrades were killed in West Bengal during the preceding three years, followed by 65 in Kerala, 21 in Andhra Pradesh, 20 in Bihar, and 12 in Rajasthan. In retrospect, it is understandable that I should be looked at with a degree of skepticism if not suspicion. But then, for this twenty two-year-old, who had disregarded paternal advice, left her job, and returned home, to be faced with such unexpected hurdles was difficult, to say the least.

After several unsuccessful attempts, I finally made contact with the Party. I met Biman Bose, who was then a popular and well-known student leader of the West Bengal Provincial Student Federation. I was nervous at that first meeting, but before he quizzed me, Bimanda put me at ease, offering me tea and delicious hot samosas. He introduced me to Comrade Promode Dasgupta (known as PDG), the legendary secretary of the West Bengal Party. He was known to be the steely organiser who built a Party capable of facing the anti-communist terror. He used to smoke a cheroot. When I first met him, I saw him through a cloud of smoke. PDG spent quite some time speaking to me, asking me about my background. I told him, rather hesitantly, that I would like to work among the working class. He didn't seem impressed and asked me to come back after a few days. It was like an unstated interview. At my second meeting with him, PDG asked me to go back to university and work in a student organisation on campus. 'We can decide based on your work among students whether we want you, and you can decide on the basis of your experience whether you want us'.

Honestly, I hated the idea of going back to university, having lived the life of an independent working woman for four years. But I had no choice and did as I was told. I found that PDG was right. The training I got in the university unit of the Party, working with a diverse group of young, energetic, and committed comrades, was invaluable. Our work in the university was under the leadership of Sudarshan Ray Choudhury. Sudarshanda, as he was known, was a gentle and caring person and a sharp Marxist intellectual who later became a member of parliament and a minister in the Left Front government. In those turbulent times, when everything was so new to me when I was trying to adjust my life and my thinking to the discipline required of a communist worker, I sometimes floundered and was helped by the camaraderie of the university unit and the sage advice of Sudarshanda.

I earned my party membership with a recommendation from the student branch in 1971. I was twenty-three years old. I am proud that I earned my membership in West Bengal during a tumultuous period of the Party's history. Fifty-two years later, I remain in touch with many of my comrades of the time.

From Calcutta to Delhi

I worked in the Party for five years in Calcutta, from 1970 to 1975. I met my hero, Comrade Jyoti Basu. He was a revered and beloved mass leader, and there was not a trace of arrogance in his dealings with the young cadre. He had a sardonic sense of humour. 'This is quite different from the education your father may have had in mind for you', he once said to me with a twinkle in his eye.

I treasure those years because they laid the foundation of my future work. It was the steepest learning curve, as the Party was under severe repression. In the university, too, we faced several attacks by the Congress and the left extremist groups. I was actively involved in area-based work under the local committee in the university area. I also worked in *People's Democracy*, the Party's weekly English newspaper. But my desire was to do trade union work among the working class. However, given the organisational and political circumstances in West Bengal at the time, I realised this was not going to be possible. P. Sundarayya was then the General Secretary of the Party. He would often attend meetings of *People's Democracy*. He knew what I really wanted. One day, he called me to his office. 'If you are serious about working on the trade union front, I suggest you shift to Delhi. I have spoken to Jaipal. He is sensitive and sympathetic to young women cadre. It always helps when the Party leader takes a special interest in the development of young women cadre.' He was referring to Major Jaipal Singh, who was at the time the secretary of the Delhi Party. He was affectionately called 'Comrade Major'.

P. Sundarayya (or simply PS) was a brilliant leader and a remarkable human being. He had been one of the principal leaders of the Telangana peasants' armed revolt against the oppressive feudal lords and their benefactor, the colonial state. He had worked closely with Comrade Major, who had been one of the military commanders in the Telangana revolt. PS himself was known to take a keen interest in the development of young cadres. Student leaders of the time recall how PS knew the names and other details of numerous student cadres all over India. He used to carry a small notebook in which, among other things, he would jot down names of young activists. He would monitor their progress from time to time.

PS's words ring true even decades later. It is easier for young women to combat patriarchal trends in society and within the Party when the leading functionary, in most cases the secretary, is sensitive and aware of the social and infrastructural support a woman activist requires.

My shift to Delhi was finalised. As it happened, my desire to work on the trade union front was not to be realised in ordinary times but during the Emergency when open trade union activity was banned. That was how I found myself in that clandestine meeting in the darkened office room in Kamla Nagar.

A 'Party Wedding'

I got married within six months of my shift to Delhi. I met Prakash when he visited Calcutta as the national president of the Students' Federation of India (SFI). We met again in Delhi, and our relationship developed — two wholetimers of the Party, young and idealistic. We had a discussion as to whether we should formalise our relationship by getting married. The Emergency, when so many of our comrades were in jail, was hardly the ideal time for a wedding. Prakash consulted Comrade Surjeet, who smiled and said in that case he should forget about getting married at all, as there was no telling how long the Emergency would last. But he did warn us that we may have the police as unwanted guests! We decided to get married and chose 7 November as our wedding day — the anniversary of the Russian Revolution.

The problem of a venue for a wedding where the groom is semi-underground and when both the bride and groom are living under aliases — Prakash as Sudhir and me as Rita — was solved by the generosity of Dr Vina Mazumdar, who opened her home for us. Her daughters Indrani and Shashwati were students at JNU, and Prakash had met her through them. He warned her that the police may turn up. She was undeterred and joked about how she had dealt with more than a couple of policemen in her life. That was the first time I met her. I had no idea then what an important influence she was to become in my life.

Our guest list was naturally restricted, given the circumstances. The bridal side consisted of my sisters, Junie and Radha, brother-in-law Prannoy, and two naughty nieces, Shonali (aged nine) and Atiya (five). Prakash's mother and a few of our mutual friends made up the gathering of about twenty people. Among them was my friend Madhu. She had started teaching at Delhi University (DU) by the time I got to Delhi. There, she met and later married Rajendra Prasad, an excellent organiser who was among the founders of the SFI in DU. Prakash and he were good friends, and Madhu had been my roommate in the college hostel. They were both present at our clandestine wedding, as was Suneet, and Rajen had, in fact, taken up some organisational responsibilities even here! The artist Vivan Sundaram was there with his camera. The wedding photographs in this book are by him. Another special guest was Appan Menon. He was perhaps Prakash's closest friend. He was extremely warm and affable and went on to become an ace journalist. I think it was Appan who presented Prakash with his Kerala-style wedding dress, a crisp white mundu and a spotless white shirt.

We were fortunate that the legendary communist leader Comrade A.K. Gopalan, or AKG, and his life partner, Susheela, herself a trade union and women's leader, were present in Delhi at the time. They, along with Comrade Surjeet, presided over the wedding. The guests made themselves comfortable sitting on rugs neatly arranged by Vinadi.

Prakash and I had separately written our pledges to each other and to the cause of revolution, and we read them out and exchanged garlands. AKG and Surjeet then made speeches, wishing us well. AKG put his arm around my shoulder during his speech. 'If this young man ever bothers you, come to me', he said, much to the merriment of those present. Comrade Surjeet spoke of Karl Marx and Jenny and the many sacrifices they had made for the cause of the working class and socialism. He said, 'Jenny Marx was the ideal communist wife'; I surreptitiously looked at Prakash. He knew how I would respond to this and kept his eyes firmly fixed on Comrade Surjeet. No, I had no intention of being an 'ideal wife' —communist or otherwise!

Just as the ceremony concluded, Atiya, with a cheeky smile, suddenly popped up in front of Prakash and held out a silver

Rita and Sudhir — Brinda and Prakash — get married on 7 November 1975, anniversary of the Russian Revolution, at Dr Vina Mazumdar's home. The artist Vivan Sundaram, who took these wedding photographs, captured the 'sindoor moment' when Rita's niece Atiya surprised Sudhir.

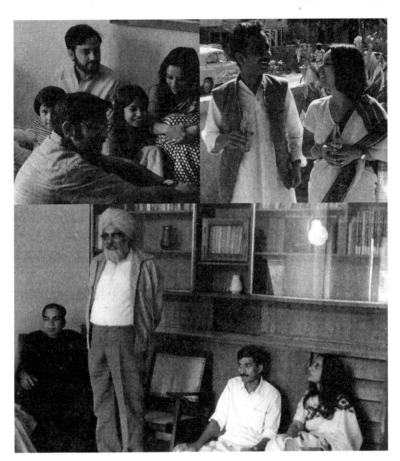

Wedding guests: Prannoy and Radhika Roy, Shonali, Atiya, Suneet Chopra; Rajendra and Madhu Prasad; H.K.S. Surjeet speaks of Jenny and Marx as A.K. Gopalan looks on; Amma and Susheela Gopalan.

container with vermilion powder — sindoor, the mark of a married woman. Prakash looked me straight in the eye. He knew I disliked women-only marriage symbols. However, to avoid a scene, I nodded consent, and he dipped his finger in the powder and gingerly applied a dot of red to the parting of my hair. Atiya had been prompted by Junie, determined to have a touch of Bengal in the proceedings. It was the first and last time I wore sindoor!

The first 'Party wedding' I ever attended was my own. Since then, I have been to hundreds of such weddings where young people, without huge expenses and without elaborate religious rituals, including patriarchal ones like kanyadaan — the 'gifting' of one's daughter to the groom — signal an alternative culture by getting married in a simple, dignified, and meaningful way. I did, of course, have to treat my comrades from the textile union to some nice mithai — and received their blessings in return.

From that day till today, our pledge has held fast — to the Party, to our work, and to each other. Prakash has always been there for me, through thick and thin, like a rock, without ever interfering in any aspect of my work.

My Lifeline

In social life, it is not easy for a young single woman to make her way in a world she is unfamiliar with.

I have been fortunate to have the support of my family, who, while not being involved with my work, have always been my lifeline. For the first few years in Calcutta, I stayed with Junie till I shifted to my rented accommodation. My elder brother, who was a manager in a tea estate in north Bengal, would come often to visit me, encouraging me in my work. Within two years of my joining the Party, my father, seeing that I was firmly set on my path, helped me financially, though on a very strict budget. When he was reconciled to my work, he found nice things to say about the Party. He told me that he preferred to deal with 'CPI (M) unions', because although the leaders were the toughest in their fight for workers' demands, once they reached an agreement, they were honest in implementing it. 'You know where you stand with them', he would say. When I decided to accept PS's suggestion to shift to Delhi, I had the confidence to do so, knowing that my younger sister Radhika and her husband Prannoy would also be living in Delhi. For years, their flat was a second home for Prakash and me.

Tragedy befell our family twice in those years. In 1978, my brother Koko was admitted to a small hospital in Jorhat, Assam, near the tea garden where he worked. He had typhoid and had to be administered glucose intravenously. The glucose bottle was possibly contaminated, and he developed a reaction which took his life. Then, in 1986, my sister Junie died in a Bombay hospital, the result of a botched surgical intervention for an intestinal obstruction. Both these deaths were likely a result of medical negligence.

Koko.

I feel their loss every day. The pain is raw and acute, even all these decades later. What is the colour of grief? Sometimes, it is a stark black and white, sometimes a softer sepia, but no matter its shape and size, it is omnipresent. Radhika and Prannoy helped to rebuild our family. They truly have been my lifeline. We became emotionally like a joint family for all the children and grandchildren. Joy and laughter fills the house at family gatherings, and we enjoy watching the younger generations grow and find their callings. I can say without hesitation that the most precious gift that life has given me has been the support and understanding of our family.

Rita and Junie.

I mention family support because I have seen the bravery and courage of many young women who join the Left in the teeth of continued opposition from their parents and siblings. I was recently at a youth convention when a young woman from Haryana showed me an abusive message from her father asking her how she had dared to attend a convention without his permission. She was in tears. For single young women in any profession, the lack of family support is often an enormous hurdle to cross. I have seen how, in Delhi, students and young people help each other in such situations since there is no other infrastructural support. At the time of the Emergency, such a solidarity network was not available to me, given that I had little connection with our comrades here — all the more reason to recall how lucky I am because of the support of my family.

Looking back, I can say that the decade as Rita was the most educative phase of my life — experiencing class struggle at the mill gate; learning how to organise a strike; getting introduced to working-class cultures and ways of life in workers' colonies; and learning of the lives and identities of women in working-class families. I experienced how bonds are formed in the crucible of

35

struggle, solidarity, comradeship, and courage. I also learnt hard lessons — of betrayals; of union breaking; of the viciousness of the management-supported strike breakers. I experienced the painful blows of police batons; the harassment of police cases; and the difficulties of prison life. None of this would have been possible without the help and support of workers and their unions.

This was also the period when I became involved with working among women, first with working-class women and subsequently as part of the team that founded a women's organisation in Delhi.

II

DELHI

Delhi's Textile Mills

There were five composite textile mills in Delhi in 1975, where all processes involved in cloth production were under one roof. Three of these were in north Delhi. The largest, Delhi Cloth Mills (DCM), was located in the Manakpura Sabzi Mandi area, near the elegant but now decrepit Art Deco cinema hall of Filmistan. About five kilometres north of DCM, if you went past Filmistan, leaving Azad Market on the right, to Kamla Nagar, you came to Birla Mills. From here, a further five kilometres north up G.T. Karnal Road, you would get to Ajudhia Textile Mills (pronounced 'Ayodhya' by most people, and, in fact, workers referred to it as ATM, which is what I'll be referring to it as here) at the busy Azadpur tri-junction. This mill had shut down but was opened again in 1972 after a prolonged struggle by workers led to its nationalisation. Despite the distance between the mills, and despite the lack of modern communication devices such as mobile phones, news of an incident at any of these mills spread to the others with surprising swiftness. The other two mills, the Swatantra Bharat Mills and DCM Silk Mills were in the Moti Nagar area in west Delhi.

Around the mills were the workers' colonies. Some colonies were constructed by the mill owners, but these accommodated a limited number of workers. Many workers rented accommodation in private colonies around the mills. Others lived in jhuggies or shacks in ramshackle, overcrowded bastis with minimal infrastructure. For instance, the basti along the railway line in Azadpur was home to hundreds of workers of ATM.

Textile workers were the heart, if not the spine, of the working-class movement in Delhi. In large measure, this had to do with the nature of industrialisation in Delhi — the five textile mills employed roughly half of all workers in large industrial enterprises in Delhi, and the city had relatively few medium-sized factories (employing 300 workers or more). The vast majority of industrial units in Delhi were small, employing less than a hundred workers. Unionising these workers was — and remains — extremely difficult. In that period of the mid-and late-1970s, many of the workers I met in the industrial areas were young, first-generation workers, migrants from rural areas of UP, Bihar and other neighbouring states to Delhi. Typically, they travelled for employment to Delhi through a relative or neighbour in their village already living here, but basically, they were on their own. Their living quarters were small rooms often shared by five or six workers. They barely eked out a living as their wages were often below the legal minimum wage. Among this section of workers, CITU was often a pioneering force as it required a great deal of effort and sustained work to organise them. As soon as owners got wind of the unionising, the workers were summarily dismissed. So, we found different ways to organise. Often, we would choose a tea shop where workers would stop on their way to work or after the workday was over. A group of us would discuss their work and then point out how they were being exploited. The effort had to be regular, at least four or five times a week at the same time, so workers came to know about the union and the organisers. We also distributed leaflets in industrial areas with the address of the Kamla Nagar office. Any registered union has the right to represent workers in labour conciliation proceedings. So we started representing workers through the CITU-affiliated General Mazdoor Lal Jhanda Union and gained their confidence.

In the textile mills, it was easier to organise as there were thousands of workers under one roof. There were many unions, at least seven, affiliated to different trade union centres in the textile mills. Some were directly affiliated to political parties, such as the union affiliated to the Congress party, the Indian National Trade Union Congress (INTUC). Most unions were not directly affiliated to a political party, even though their leaders were. In the case of the CPI(M), the Party cadre worked in multiple unions across sectors. The main aim of our work in CITU was to sharpen the class struggle against capitalist exploitation, while organising workers on their day-to-day demands. In the textile industry in Delhi, there were no department-based unions. This was advantageous to us, as such unions tend to help management pit workers of one department against those of others. However, there were 'works committees' formed for every department, which had elected members so that any specific problem of that department could be taken to the management through a process. For example, if there was a problem in the spinning department, the works committee member elected from that department would represent the problems to the management. The works committee elections were held once every two or three years. All unions would participate in these elections with candidates in different departments. Sometimes, there would be mutual agreement between two or three unions to fight the elections together, just as in the general political arena, political parties make alliances. However, when it came to negotiations after a strike, it was the leadership of unions which used to form the negotiating party.

When united in struggle, textile workers were a formidable force. This was apparent in the number of textile workers' industrial actions through the fifties and sixties. Workers became even more conscious of their rights in the early 1970s after many unions affiliated themselves with the newly formed CITU, breaking the stranglehold of the more reformist unions which had thus far dominated the textile industry. In 1970–71, there was a militant strike in all the mills, which one of the reformist leaders tried to break. He was surrounded by striking workers, paraded in a massive procession, his face blackened, abused as a management agent. Workers still spoke about this incident many years later.

Solidarities, Positive and Negative

Workers developed a working-class identity while working together in the mills and by living together in workers' colonies and bastis. Under neo-liberal policies, there have been qualitative changes which have fractured, perhaps irreparably, the objective material conditions in which class identities develop. Today, processes of production in most industries are divided and sub-divided via outsourcing. Consequently, there has been a fragmentation of the workforce, with concomitant reflections at the level of culture and ideas. Mills and the surrounding workers' colonies have been bulldozed and handed over to real estate developers, who have made massive profits by turning these into gated communities, luxury residences, malls, showrooms, and shopping centres. The disappearance of labour colonies from the urban landscape has been accompanied by the dispersal of workers and labourers, undermining their political weight and weakening their striking power. Traditional working-class politics, based on worker mobilisations around the work processes and the workplace, have been weakened, whether in the economy or in cultural and social life. This has helped the rise of divisive, sectarian, identity-based politics. Caste ideologies and communal thinking have made deep inroads into different sections of the working people. It is not as though caste and communal thinking were absent in earlier times, but there were countervailing ideologies and mobilisations which were also strong.

In all my years of work in the trade union, I did not witness any overt casteism among the workers, although there were regional groupings and loyalties. I should qualify and explain what I mean. I use the word overt deliberately, as it did not mean that casteism had disappeared. While working-class consciousness and solidarity did exist and were powerful, they did not extend to every aspect of their lives. Most of the workers in the unions I worked in were from Uttar Pradesh and Bihar. When they went back to their villages, the workers from dominant castes did not challenge the caste discrimination so rampant where they lived. They would share bread with their fellow workers who were Dalit but would be horrified at the very thought of one of their daughters getting married to a Dalit worker. When we raised this issue in discussions, they would say that they were hardly home long enough to make a change. But clearly, casteism, though muted in the mills and even in residential colonies, was very much a part of their lives. The resilience of the caste system and casteist beliefs underlined in my experience the importance of organised and conscious ideological struggle against the caste system by trade unions.

In the unions affiliated with CITU, there was a mix of workers from different castes. In the weaving departments, a large section of the workers belonged to the Koli caste, a Scheduled Caste (SC) community traditionally associated with handloom weaving. The Birla Mills management was from Rajasthan, and preferred to hire workers, especially security guards, from that state. Most of them belonged to the dominant castes. The management encouraged a regional grouping of workers from Rajasthan, who, therefore, felt a sense of indebtedness towards the management.

Our union in ATM, on the other hand, was comprised predominantly of workers belonging to Scheduled Castes from eastern UP and Bihar. Many lived in bastis along the railway line in Azadpur. They were a committed, politically conscious force in the union and its leadership. It is significant that the seats won by the Communist Party of India (CPI) in Delhi's electoral politics, one in the Metropolitan Council and one in the Municipal Corporation, were from constituencies that had a concentration of textile mill workers. The corporation seat was won by the CPI leader Guru Radha Kishan several times. Working together inside mills, commuting to work and back, sharing food in the canteen, and taking part in cultural festivals and sports events created bonds between workers across regions, religions, and castes forging a shared working-class identity.

Comrades

In the years of the Emergency, 1975 to 1977, my responsibility was to work with the Birla Mills unit and in workers' colonies stretching up to ATM. The CITU-affiliated union — the Kapda Mazdoor Lal Jhanda Union — represented workers of all the five mills. The working committee meetings of the union gave me an opportunity to meet union leaders from the other mills. The DCM unit was affected as the main leader, Nathu Parshad, had been arrested during the Emergency. I worked closely with him in subsequent years, and he continues to be a senior leader of our Party in Delhi. The year Koko died, Nathu Parshad came to me on Rakhi day and handed me a red thread to tie around his wrist, a brother's symbolic gesture of support and solidarity. I will never forget that moving gesture.

DCM Silk and Swatantra Bharat mills in west Delhi were adjacent to each other, and they had an advanced group of worker leaders. The CITU union functioned from an office in Karampura, about a 15-minute walk from the mill gates. The leaders here, such as Inder Pal, Rammurti, Roshanlal, and Vasu, were experts in labour law and knew every nuance of each department in the mills and the processes of production. They were from different regions — Roshan Lal, the oldest, was from Punjab; Inder Pal, an able organiser, was from eastern UP; Rammurti was from western UP; and Vasu was from Kerala. They worked well as a team. They were better than any educated, trained lawyer. It was fascinating to hear them speak in the meetings of the working committee on various issues confronting the workers. Every time I learnt something new. I learnt from them how the management, in cahoots with some unions, would resort to its usual tactic to end an agitation: it

Rita with her comrades of the Kapda Mazdoor Lal Jhanda Union. On the extreme right (bespectacled, holding file) is Ram Pal; to Rita's right (fist raised) is Tripurari, on his right, with his hand on another comrade's shoulder, is Inder Pal.

would refer the dispute to a committee or to the industrial tribunal, where it would linger on for years. According to them, numerous important cases relating to wage and Dearness Allowance (DA) were stuck in tribunals. Over the years, Inder Pal and I became good friends. I had great respect for his leadership qualities, his calm approach during heated discussions, and his ability to work as part of a team.

Before the Emergency, the mill gates were centres of activity. The unions would hold meetings, distribute leaflets, put up notices and posters, and talk to workers at the mill gates. The virtual ban on trade union activity now meant that all this was ruled out. We had to shift our attention to the residential colonies, meet workers in their homes, and hold meetings in secret. Between Birla Mills and ATM, and behind the middle-class colony of Pratap Bagh, was a basti called Sawan Park, where handloom workers lived.

There were almost two dozen members of the Party living in these jhuggies, all of them belonging to the Koli community. The area was considered a safe zone, and comrades here, led by Sarwan Kumar, a handloom worker, hosted many meetings of textile workers. Sarwan was an extrovert, easy to get along with, and popular in the area. He had studied only till Class 8 but was able to memorise so many statistics that it was quite amazing. I found this quality among many worker leaders who had been deprived of formal education. Comrade Puran Chand was one such leader. I met him after the Emergency when he was Secretary of the Party committee in west Delhi. He had studied only till Class 5, but he could quote the details of labour laws and their clause numbers; he could quote official statistics to make a point! In other words, worker leaders had to work twice as hard as a literate middle-class comrade. It was such realities that I was exposed to, which brought out in myriad ways, in my day-to-day experiences, the cruel inequalities of a capitalist society.

There was also a small bookshop at the corner of Roop Nagar, not far from the union office in Karampura, which also doubled up as the party office. It sold left-wing publications and was run by Comrade Kamal Narayan, a former DCM employee dismissed for his union activism. He later became general secretary of the textile union. We would also hold meetings in his shop. He would down the shutters, and we would meet in a room at the back. He was also on the police watch list, so he was also given an underground name — Doctor — since, according to the worker comrades, he looked like one! That moniker stayed with him for the rest of his life. It was Sriram who introduced me to the various party units and taught me about the industry. He once told me, 'A worker must always be an expert in the work he does, whether it is on a weaving machine or a spinning machine. Those who disrespect work and a work ethic can never develop into union leaders. Never trust a lazy worker'.

What the Workers Faced

The main issue faced by the textile workers across the five mills, though in differing degrees, was the effort of the managements to increase the workload manifold times. Even before the Emergency was declared, managements had started increasing workloads without any investment on new machinery. For example, in the DCM spinning department, the machines were 'speeded up' to produce more loaded spindles, which had to be checked by the worker within the same amount of time. So fewer workers were being asked to do more work. In other departments, too, such processes were started by the managements. A prominent DCM union leader, Sohan Lal, estimated that when he joined as a young man of 18 in 1967, there were 7,500 workers in the mill, which had come down to 5,000 by the time of the Emergency — a reduction by one-third in less than a decade! The management would give one year's wages as retrenchment 'benefit'. Moreover, textile owners in Delhi had an extremely arbitrary method of fixing wages. This was unlike mills in Bombay or Kanpur, where there was categorisation and standardisation of wages. The demand for a wage board for Delhi textile workers was an urgent and longstanding one.

Dearness allowance was a major issue. In India, even before Independence, the government would pay its employees a percentage of the basic salary linked to the consumer price index to curb the impact of inflation. This right, however, was limited to the government sector, and did not extend to workers and employees in the private sector. After many struggles, workers in different industries, such as textile, succeeded in getting recognition for the right to dearness allowance through various industrial tribunals. A significant one was known as the 1973

Vaidyalingam Award, named after its chairman, which mandated that mills should pay workers 90 per cent DA for total working days. The managements interpreted this to mean 90 per cent of the days worked by each worker, not the days that the mill was in operation, as was the original intention of the award. Effectively, this represented a reduction of 12 per cent, and the workers were paid only 78 per cent DA. An *India Today* report from 1979 (at the time of the strike) estimated that 'The difference amounts to Rs 25 a month per worker, or Rs 72 lakh per year. But this small bone of contention, has cost the workers' wages worth Rs 4.75 crore and caused the country a production loss of Rs 19 crore'.

Then there was the issue of workers' health. The architecture of the mills was such that the shop floors where workers worked were windowless, with high skylights. The air would be full of cotton fluff, which the workers would constantly breathe in since the management didn't provide masks, nor was mask-wearing considered a part of the standard protocol. Workers in the dyeing department would often get burn injuries from chemicals and acids, but the management wouldn't provide protective gear or other safety equipment. In department after department, the management would refuse to spend any money on improving working conditions. To be sure, workers were part of the Employees' State Insurance (ESI) scheme, which technically gave them easy access to health benefits. In reality, however, the quality of health care accessible to workers remained poor, and in any case, poor working conditions meant a disproportionately large proportion of workers fell ill frequently. Tuberculosis was particularly rampant.

Discontent among workers was growing, and mobilisations on these issues had already begun when the Emergency was declared.

STRIKE!

The flashpoint came in Birla Mills. Workers here had a reputation of militancy. In early 1976, the management took the decision to ask each worker to work four looms instead of two. They were enabled by a decision of the labour court, the D.D. Gupta Award, which supported the management's contention that the increased workload was required for increasing productivity. The award also gave the management permission to work the mill round the clock, seven days a week. The management made its intentions known to the workers. There was anger among the workers at this unfair increase in workload. The union comrades reported that workers were asking them to 'do something'. We started holding secret meetings of the workers. We had a good team in the weaving department, so we were able to cover all the shifts. A leader was elected in each shift, and the workers decided that the protest had to start at the machine itself.

On the night of 18 April 1976, the management put its plan into action. The supervisor of the night shift informed the workers that the four-loom system was to start immediately and pointed to one set of looms where it was to start. The next set was where the CITU shift leader, Harish Chandra Pant was working. Comrade Pant told us later that the first worker was pressurised by the supervisor, who shouted instructions next to him to start working the four looms. Pant was next in line. He stood in front of his machine, arms outstretched, and shouted, 'Strike, strike! We will not accept this workload!' This brave action had an electrifying effect. Other workers gathered around him and shouted slogans. The strike was on. Harish Chandra Pant made history that day. Pant, still active in the CITU in Delhi, was from the hilly regions of

Striking presence — Harish Chandra Pant in 1976.

Uttarakhand. He was brought to Delhi at the age of sixteen by his elder brother, a worker in the Birla Mills. In a few years, unlike his elder brother, the young Pant, angered by the terrible conditions of work, joined the CITU union. When I met him, he was an office bearer of the Birla Mills unit.

It was the first such workers' action during the Emergency in the textile industry in Delhi — perhaps even the first across all sectors in Delhi. Word spread through all departments, and workers started coming out, gathering inside the mill premises. The strike also had a political impact. A Congress minister, speaking in the Metropolitan Council (Delhi didn't have a Legislative Assembly at the time), lamented that the strike in the capital had lowered the prestige of the Council by running contrary to its steadfast support to the Emergency in the national interest!

In the preparatory phase leading up to the action, I often stayed overnight in the home of one of our comrades, Ramesh, a worker in the weaving department. He had rented quarters close to the mill. He stayed with his wife, Manju, his two young boys, and his mother, Omvati.

I was witness to and participated in detailed discussions among the workers on the pros and cons of the strike. I saw how, in meetings, union leaders listened patiently to all sides of the argument. On occasion, one of our Party leaders, Umesh Mishra, who was a lawyer by profession, also attended these meetings. He would also listen with care to the workers' opinions. The atmosphere in these meetings was open, frank, and democratic, and leaders, far from issuing orders, encouraged discussion. One section of the workers felt that the administration would call in the police and break the strike violently. The other section felt that the government would want to avoid any negative publicity that police violence would bring because Delhi is the capital, and action here would have repercussions in the rest of the country. Some workers felt that the weaving department would get isolated since workers from other departments were not directly affected and would not support a prolonged strike. Someone asked, how can we ensure the success of the strike since the police would not allow picket lines at the gate? This was a crucial issue since a strong picket line with many workers gives confidence to other workers that they are not alone and that it would be difficult for the management to penalise them for joining the strike if large numbers took part in it. We, therefore, identified all the approaches to the mill gate that workers used and decided to set up a series of picket lines on them. Workers also discussed the role of other unions. There was consensus that we could not depend on them and that we must build our own independent strength and be responsive to the mood of the workers. We drafted a leaflet that explained how retrenchment was the inevitable consequence of the increased workload that workers were confronting. There was such an atmosphere of fear that no printer agreed to print the leaflet. We had to cyclostyle it. (Cyclostyling is now an extinct technology. It used to be quite laborious and slow — imagine each leaflet being printed using a stencil sheet). Union members would carry the leaflet into the mill surreptitiously and would leave a copy or two at each machine. I heard how workers were carefully folding the leaflet and keeping it in their pockets for later perusal. This quiet act alone was enough to tell us that there was growing support among workers for the strike. Clearly, our campaign was on the right track.

Ramesh, who was on the morning shift that day, got the news of the strike at night. I was there that night. We put into action our plan to station ourselves at different points along the various approaches to the mill in place of a single picket line at the gate. At 5 in the morning, I stood in one of the lanes from the workers' colony with a group of striking workers. We had to ensure that workers on the 5.30 am shift returned home rather than go into the mill. I realised that we did not have much time. Comrades felt if we persuaded the first group walking to the mill to turn back, the job would be done. That is precisely what happened. Hardly any workers challenged us. They dispersed silently, knowing that the police could appear any minute. It was an inspirational moment for me to see scores of workers turning back, nodding their approval, some with a clenched fist raised in solidarity.

The strike lasted seven days. As anticipated by workers in our preparatory meetings, workers in the other departments not directly affected started asking the union to withdraw the strike. Other unions were also campaigning against the strike, telling workers it was not in their interests. On the third day of the strike, a supervisor conveyed to Sriram that the management was prepared to talk, but on two conditions — that only he negotiate and that the meeting remain confidential till an agreement was reached. Sriram reported this to the others. Normally, in CITU, we did not approve of a single leader negotiating with the management. Negotiations should always be done by a team. In this instance, however, comrades felt that an exception should be made, given the complex and challenging situation we faced.

Sriram went for the meeting alone. The management made the following offer: the increased workload would remain, but for each thread broken on the two extra looms which the worker had to repair, he would be paid compensation. Many of us felt it was a ridiculous offer for three reasons. One, accepting it meant accepting the increased workload with no countervailing assurance that workers wouldn't be retrenched. Two, it was practically impossible to keep track of broken threads. Three, even if a worker somehow kept count, what prevented supervisors from disputing his claim? But Sriram himself was in favour of accepting the offer, as were some others. The workers were divided.

P. Ramamurthi was then the all-India general secretary of CITU. Comrade PR, as he was called, was a vastly experienced leader. He had been a freedom fighter since the 1920s and a trade unionist since the 1930s. He was elected to the Madras legislative assembly and subsequently to the Lok Sabha. He had taken a personal interest in the agitation and was following developments on a day-to-day basis. I asked for his advice. He said he would come to the union general body meeting. He listened to the opinions of everybody who spoke and said if the CITU-affiliated union signed such an agreement, it would bind the workers to an increased workload, making us responsible for the subsequent retrenchment. He felt it was better to withdraw a struggle honourably than by trying to mask a long-term defeat as a short-term victory. Workers applauded spontaneously and warmly at the end of his speech.

They appreciated this stand. They felt that the strike was not a defeat ; it was a show of strength.

The lesson I drew from this experience was that it is imperative for workers to have a voice and a say in the decisions taken during a struggle, particularly involving a strike. They should be, in fact, as well as perception, participants in the decision-making process. If unions take decisions at the leadership level and only communicate these to workers, as reformist unions do, it leaves the workers disappointed and demoralised. This sets back the class struggle.

The strike was called off. Pant was suspended. There was much propaganda against us. The management openly stated that it had taught 'CITU a lesson'. Not long after the strike, elections for the Works Committee were held. The CITU union did exceptionally well, winning all the seats in the weaving department and some in other departments, too. The management was shocked. They had held elections only because they believed that after the withdrawal of the strike, CITU would be defeated. Pant was reinstated some months later, though without his wages. After the strike, he, Ramesh, and others were recognised as leaders by the workers. The imposition of work on four looms was stopped for a while. There was no immediate retrenchment. After some time, the management opened a separate section of the weaving department where workers who agreed to work on four looms were shifted.

My work in the union was linked to my role as a communist organiser. I had been co-opted as a member of the north Delhi local committee of the Party, of which Sriram was the secretary. The Party organised many campaigns against the Emergency. We wanted to tell the world that people were not timid and quiescent but were actively resisting the Emergency. We would distribute leaflets at night in residential areas where workers lived. We would also leave a bunch of leaflets at public places. A particularly favourite spot was on the overbridge across the railway line near DCM. We would sometimes watch from a distance as workers would surreptitiously pick up a leaflet, fold it, and keep it in their pocket to read later in private. We also wrote slogans and messages on walls. These 'wall writing' campaigns would be done late at night by teams of three comrades each. To save time and effort, workers would make tin stencils with simple words cut out — *virodh* (opposition), *Emergency murdabad* (down with the Emergency), *Inquilab zindabad* (Long Live the Revolution), and so on. One comrade would carry the paint; the other would quickly stencil the slogan on the wall using a brush; the third would be the lookout for the police. It was a thrilling experience, which I enjoyed a lot — also because, fortunately, we never got caught!

Amma

A few weeks after we were married, Prakash and I rented a small two-room outhouse in Model Town. We could at last bring Amma, Prakash's mother, out of the solitary existence that the Emergency had forced her into.

I want to introduce my ever-smiling, loving mother-in-law to you with the story of my first meeting with her. Prakash had made a secret trip to Vithalbhai Patel House (V.P. House), the hostel for members of parliament where the two of them had lived. He told her about our decision to get married. A few days later, I went to see Amma. She welcomed me with her beautiful smile, held out her arms and enveloped me in a warm hug. I said, 'Amma, I know you will be disappointed that your daughter-in-law is not from Kerala and cannot speak Malayalam'. She laughed. 'That is not my worry at all. I just wish you two to be happy'. She suffered from rheumatoid arthritis, and it was only months later that she told me that, that day, she had been in excruciating pain. I would never have imagined.

Prakash was the centre of Amma's life, and he, in turn, was deeply attached to her. They had lost Prakash's elder sister, Kamla, possibly of tetanus, when she was thirteen years old. They were living in Burma at the time, where Prakash's father was employed with the railways. Four years later, Prakash's father died of a heart attack. Now, Prakash was thirteen years old. I once asked Amma how she had coped during those difficult years. 'What could I have done — I had to be practical and work out ways so that Prakash and I could survive'.

She pulled herself out of her sorrow. She became an insurance agent so she could earn enough to raise Prakash. She sold her small

Amma, Rita, Junie and the children on Rita's wedding day.

house in Palghat. With that money, she built a house in Chennai, which she rented out for an income. Prakash and she lived in the small adjoining outhouse. She did all this almost singlehandedly. For her to take on all these responsibilities required a great deal of strength and fortitude. She never let her problems weigh her down. As her many friends and members of her family recall, she was always smiling and cheerful.

Prakash was academically brilliant and won a scholarship. Normally, this should have paved the way for a financially successful career. Amma's hopes were belied when Prakash turned his back on money and professional success and decided instead to become a wholetime Party worker. It was A.K. Gopalan who spoke to Amma about Prakash's decision and assured her that the Party would always be there for her. I can't say if she felt disappointed. She certainly responded with her characteristic practicalness, and sold the house she had gotten built with such difficulty. She moved to Delhi to be with Prakash. His friends from the time were the beneficiaries — they were always assured of a fulsome meal or a tasty treat whenever they dropped in. She loved feeding them and developed close bonds with many of them.

The Emergency changed all this. Prakash had to go underground and shift from his room in Vitthalbhai Patel House. Amma was forced to live alone at a time when her health was failing her. It was incredibly hard for Prakash and for her. Many JNU students were arrested. Several faced myriad difficulties. It was difficult for them to visit Amma. Fortunately, there was a group of junior doctors from Kerala, friends of Prakash, who were doing their postgraduate studies in Delhi. Some of them stayed at the hostel at the All India Institute of Medical Sciences (AIIMS). Not only did they provide shelter to Prakash in the hostel on the AIIMS campus — an unlikely place for a political activist who was underground — but they often visited Amma and looked after her. I remember with affection that group of medical students, now doctors, always so helpful — Bhaskaran, Mohan, Sukumaran, and Venu.

Prakash was immensely relieved and happy that it became possible for Amma to shift from Vitthalbhai Patel House and be with us. We had lovely days together in that small, cosy flat in Model Town. Amma soon made friends with the landlady and would send delicacies that she had cooked for her family. She would tell me stories of her life in Burma and share stories about Prakash as a child, things I would never have known.

But we got very little time together. Just four months. Amma's health deteriorated. She died in early March 1976. Prakash was deeply impacted. All his friends from JNU and Amma's numerous admirers were there to bid her farewell. I loved Amma deeply. I wish we could have lived together longer. I wish I could have given her the love and care she needed.

Comrade PS

One morning soon after Amma's passing in March 1976, Prakash and I woke up to a knock on our door. We opened the door and were astonished to find Comrade P. Sundarayya standing there, smiling warmly. He had heard of Amma's death and knew how upset Prakash would be.

I have mentioned earlier how PS was such an exceptional leader, a legend in his lifetime, the foremost leader of the massive Telangana armed peasant uprising against the feudal and oppressive rule of the Nizam and landlords in Hyderabad state. It began in July 1946 on the eve of Independence and continued for five years, till 1951, before it was crushed by Nehru. At its peak, the revolt liberated nearly the entire Telangana region and created a network of village communes called *gram rajyams* that ran what was effectively a parallel government. The rajyams redistributed land among the poor and landless farmers. Under the rajyams, caste and gender exploitation were reduced, the condition of life of the peasants improved significantly, and many more women started taking part in public life, including in armed struggle.

Later, as part of my work in the women's movement, I was fortunate to come close to Comrade Mallu Swarajyam, one of the heroines of the struggle who was one of the founder members of All India Democratic Women's Association (AIDWA). She strongly believed that the focus of our struggle must be on the organisation of poor rural women and brought that perspective in the earlier debates on AIDWA's work. PS announced, to Prakash's and my delight, that he would stay with us whenever he visited Delhi. PS was then underground, and we introduced him to our landlord as Prakash's uncle.

Prakash had all-India responsibilities because of his work in the SFI and was in constant touch with the Party's central leadership. He also had some responsibilities in Delhi. I used to leave for my work quite early and would cook for PS and Prakash before leaving. One day, when I returned in the evening, I found PS squatting on the kitchen floor with Prakash, cutting vegetables and giving instructions. PS had a special, mischievous smile reserved for occasions such as this. 'I used to get tastier food in the forests of Telangana than here, so I'm going to teach you both to cook'. So, among the many things I learned from PS, whom I consider my guru, was how to make a delicious Andhra-style curry! Prakash learned a thing or two in the kitchen and shared domestic chores.

It was on one of those evenings that we got around to discussing family. Prakash and I had decided not to have children to be able to devote ourselves fully to the Party. PS shared his own story with us. He had met his wife, Leila, in the communist commune in Bombay. PS was underground, and Leila was among those managing the commune. They had decided not to have children. PS got a vasectomy done without telling Leila. He said, 'If I have one deep personal regret, it is this — even though at the time I thought Leila agreed with me, I could have mistaken the pressure of her circumstances, our difficult living conditions, for her consent. She may have changed her mind about having children, but I never gave her that chance. Leila di herself never expressed such thoughts. They had a loving relationship, caring for each other deeply, which made a deep impression on me.

PS shared so many experiences of his work with us during those visits. He once said to me, 'The role of an individual in the communist movement is important. But always remember: a leader is as tall as the Party is. If the Party does not grow, it matters little if an individual's stature grows'. Important words to recall now, especially when bourgeois parties promote cults around individuals.

He also made changes in our lifestyle — making us work out

a daily schedule which involved at least an hour or two of reading. He also advised us to make notes of what we thought was of particular relevance to our own work.

It was during the Emergency years that I read many of the Marxist classics and felt it helped my work. This was critical for my ideological education. In our present age of bytes, TikTok shorts and Instagram reels, it appears as if the vast potential of the human mind is being narrowed to an attention span of a few seconds; the importance of self-education can hardly be overemphasised. It is crucial for ideological clarity, particularly for building movements subversive of the status quo. In our Party, too, when we review our work, we find that the habit of reading is fading. For communists, grounded as we ought to be in Marxist theoretical tools and methodologies, if reading recedes, it could be terribly damaging. Marxism is not a set of beliefs that are fixed for all time to come; it is a living, dynamic analytical framework that helps us understand the ever-changing present.

Workers' Lives

My work at the time, both in the Party and on the trade union front, was concentrated on the working-class colonies stretching between the textile mills in the industrial areas of G.T. Karnal Road and Wazirpur in north Delhi. I started going to the handloom workers' colony in Sawan Park. Before the Emergency, comrades from DU would come to this area and conduct study classes for workers on Marxism. Among these comrades were Babli Gupta (formerly Nagpal) and Nina Chopra (later Rao). They were both lecturers at DU. Workers appreciated their classes. They prepared the ground for a dedicated team of comrades deeply committed to the red flag. Babli and Nina were part of a group of young women who were trained by Kitty Menon (formerly Bomla). Kitty had been a brilliant student at the London School of Economics in the early 1940s. She left a comfortable life in London to join the cause of the Indian revolution. She was one of the early young communist women members in the Bombay commune. Later, she married Ramdas Menon, a communist ideologue and organiser from Kerala who became a member of the first central committee of the CPI(M) in 1964 after the split with the CPI. Comrade Ramdas was working editor for *People's Democracy* for several years. I worked under his guidance as a young wholetimer in *People's Democracy* in Calcutta. Kitty used to hold regular study circles for young women students and lecturers. She helped build a team of ideologically committed comrades in Delhi, which helped the Party in the trying days ahead.

Nearby, there was another jhuggi area in which some workers of the Delhi Transport Corporation (DTC) lived. One of them was Ladoo Ram, a driver, who was related to Sriram. During the

Emergency, he and a few other DTC workers were our messengers who carried news and instructions between Party units across the city. We would keep a copy of Ladoo Ram's duty chart and make sure we boarded his bus on time. We would convey the message to him, and he would deliver it efficiently and accurately to the comrade at the other end. Ladoo Ram and other DTC comrades would also be couriers for a political broadsheet that was published by the Delhi CPI(M).

Since workers often got off their shifts well into the evening, we would sometimes have meetings late at night. In the handloom workers' colonies, we would meet at night after the workday was done. After such meetings, I would be dropped home by a worker comrade on his bicycle. I used to cover my head with the pallu of my sari to avoid attention. The bicycles owned by handloom workers were particularly comfortable, because their carriers had been modified to cart rolls of cotton yarn or bundles of bedsheets. One night, after the meeting, a handloom worker called Budhsen was to drop me home on his bicycle. Ladoo Ram invited us both for dinner at his house. There was no electricity when we got to his jhuggi. I could hardly make out what we were being served in the dancing dim light of the solitary lantern. But Budhsen jumped with joy — it was his favourite dish. When I peered into the pot to see what it was, a goat head stared back at me, surrounded by goat feet. Ladoo Ram saw me gasp. 'This is a delicacy, comrade — siri [head] and paya [feet].' I was hardly not going to eat it and tried to camouflage my turning stomach with praise. But Ladoo Ram was not one to be fooled. 'Oh comrade, you are like one of those vegetarian types!'

Handloom workers lived in terrible conditions. The loom sheds were their homes. Sarwan had four looms and was considered better off. Most workers had one or two looms, while some had none and worked for a wage on others' looms. Sarwan's wife Prasanni spun cotton on a spinning wheel, charkha. The charkha was the revered symbol of India's freedom struggle, but here in Sawan Park, it stood for poverty and exploitation. Dozens of women like Prasanni would sit in rows spinning their charkhas for endless hours, all for a pittance. Poverty was omnipotent — half-clad little children played between the looms; women's anaemic bodies testified to their poor diets; tuberculosis (TB) often wreaked havoc on already emaciated workers' bodies; the workers drank the water from shallow tubewells that was unfit for human consumption; jaundice was common. It was only a decade later that the living conditions improved when, after a prolonged struggle under the red flag, the residents won a reasonable settlement plan, and hundreds of households got titles to plots in the nearby Ashok Vihar.

The crisis in the textile sector, which included the handloom sector, was already apparent. The central government established an office of a Development Commissioner for the handloom sector with a special branch for Delhi. A subsidy was earmarked for the handloom sector, but neither the handloom owners nor the workers ever received it. Sarwan took the initiative in getting Weavers' Cooperative Societies registered. We spent hours helping workers fill up a myriad of complicated forms. As a result of all this, we succeeded in forming a strong handloom workers' union soon after the Emergency was lifted. Once again, under Sarwan's leadership, the cooperatives came together and formed their federation.

The 'Beautification' of Delhi

In 1976, there was another upheaval in the lives of workers. Under Sanjay Gandhi's leadership, the Congress government decided to 'beautify' Delhi by clearing jhuggis. The demolition drive was presided over by Jagmohan, who was then vice chairman of the Delhi Development Authority (DDA). Residents of the colonies that were demolished by the DDA found themselves hurled to the edges of the city. Today, the scale of that brutal 'relocation' has been forgotten. In fact, hundreds of thousands of workers were forcibly evicted from their dwellings, which were demolished, and the land levelled. I'm not sure if there's been a mass eviction on this scale anywhere in India or even the world. Underlying Sanjay Gandhi's violent beautification drive was a brute reality — the value of land — real estate — far outweighed the value of poor workers' lives. This was decades before the advent of economic reform — the misleading term used for the set of policies of aggressive neo-liberalism which normalised such actions.

Take the case of Turkman Gate at the edge of the Walled City of Delhi. Many of the families had stayed in the area since Mughal times. Relocation would have meant a complete uprooting of economic and social ties that went back centuries. On 18 April 1976, the police swooped in, arresting several protestors and, when that was not enough to break the resistance, firing at them. The residents of that colony bravely resisted the bulldozers. There had been no official acknowledgement of how many people were killed in this firing, and the press censorship meant that journalists could not report either. But it is generally believed that at least six were killed, maybe more. 'Turkman Gate' became a sort of shorthand to refer to the terrible repression that was unleashed across Delhi on the poor. Industrial workers, domestic workers, street vendors, manual labourers, daily wagers — anybody living in the targeted jhuggi colonies found their dwellings, their meagre belongings, bulldozed. They were given slips that told them where they were to be relocated. A large number were forced to shift east across the river to what was called Yamuna-paar (trans-Yamuna) 'resettlement colonies', far away from their places of work.

Jagmohan's career is a telling example of the complete unanimity among India's bourgeois political parties vis-à-vis attitudes towards the poor. He was handsomely rewarded by three separate — and ideologically mutually-opposed — dispensations for his hatchet job on the poor. During the Emergency, he was part of the inner coterie of Sanjay Gandhi. The Congress rewarded him with the lieutenant governorship of first Goa and then Delhi. He was awarded the Padma Shri as well as the Padma Bhushan. When the Janata Dal-led United Front government replaced the Congress, he became governor of Jammu and Kashmir. He subsequently joined the Bharatiya Janata Party (BJP) in 1995, thrice representing that party in parliament and serving as minister in Atal Bihari Vajpayee's government. The Modi government rewarded him for his vociferous support of the abrogation of Article 370, that had conferred special status to Jammu and Kashmir, with the Padma Vibhushan in 2016. Honest officers who work to protect the rights of the poor backed by constitutional and legal frameworks very rarely, if ever, get such rewards. They are more likely to be at the receiving end of punishment postings. I have met many officers in the IAS (Indian Administrative Services) who join the services to be of some help to the poor but often end up disillusioned. In today's India, it is much worse. The 'iron framework' of governance has melted, and officers are suborned to serve the interests of the ruling BJP.

In areas where I worked in north Delhi, too, thousands of houses were razed to rubble. We got desperate messages for help from the workers. The first 'resettlement colony' I went to was

Nand Nagri in north east Delhi, near Shahdara. If you went to the crowded and bustling colony of Nand Nagri today, it would be hard for you to imagine the sight I saw back in 1976. It was a vast, barren plain with not a tree in sight. The scalding wind of the brutal Delhi summer whipped up dust from which there was no escape. Our faces and clothes, and the meagre belongings of the desolate families, would all be full of dust. Thirsty children howled as desperate mothers hunted for non-existent water sources. It was a nightmare.

At the other end of the city, in north Delhi, was Jahangirpuri, another 'resettlement colony'. The situation here was like the one in Nand Nagri. Thousands of workers and jhuggi dwellers were simply dumped here. Many of them were poor Muslims who had migrated to Delhi from Bengal. Almost all were daily wage earners who had set up their jhuggis on the banks of the Yamuna, from where they were shifted to Block C of Jahangirpuri. Their condition was absolutely appalling. They had no savings. No one was prepared to give them loans. They were treated in an extremely callous manner by officials. Decades later, in April 2022, poor Muslim residents of Jahangirpuri again faced the wrath of bulldozers, this time under the BJP government and administration, giving no heed even to a Supreme Court order. My Party and I had to physically intervene by standing in front of the bulldozers, waving the court order, which was being violated with complete impunity by the administration. There was a difference, though, a crucial one. In 1976, when the eviction drive started, it was not targeting citizens on the basis of their religion — and secondly, those evicted did get alternative land. Today, the evictions and the bulldozers are almost always targeted at minority community citizens in a blatantly communal manner.

Back in 1976, Delhi's poor faced the savage brutality and inhumanity of capitalist development as best they could. Almost everybody I met had to take loans at exorbitant rates of interest just to be able to shift to the barren landscape that was to be their new

Jahangirpuri, April 2022. Brinda stands in front of a municipal corporation bulldozer demolishing the shops and homes of poor Muslims in violation of a Supreme Court order.

home. They had to hire vans to shift their belongings; they had to build temporary jhuggis to have a roof over their heads; children had to find admission in new schools or drop out of education altogether; women had to find work as domestic labour near the resettlement colonies; men had to commute to their places of work, often twenty or thirty kilometres away. Hundreds of thousands of people, already poor, were pushed deeper into poverty. Factory and mill owners benefited, though, because workers were now totally preoccupied with the cruel fallout of evictions, diverting their attention from the union and the collective struggle.

In the Party, we redivided our work responsibilities, and many of us started going regularly to resettlement colonies. I used to go to Nand Nagri and Jahangirpuri, at two ends of the city. It was not just physically exhausting but also emotionally draining. I was filled with rage at the callousness of the government and even more at our own helplessness. The relief we provided was utterly inadequate, given the enormity of the problem. Soon, the monsoon arrived, and the rains made everything worse. Diseases and ailments such as typhoid, jaundice, and various fevers became common. We did what we could by getting the local authorities to arrange for water tankers. But it was a bit like applying a band-aid to a severed limb.

We had agitated at the time for the plot holders to be given ownership rights. That didn't happen. It also took several years for the colonies to get basic amenities such as running water and covered drainage. Many of the original residents found their lives disrupted — remember, the new resettlement colonies were a long distance away from their erstwhile homes — and sold their plots to return to their villages. In the absence of freehold rights, these sales were conducted via 'power of attorney' documents, which meant that malpractices and underhand dealings were common. Over time, some parts of the resettlement colonies (especially those closer to the main roads) became gentrified to an extent. The immense human suffering could have been avoided, and the aim of 'beautification' fulfilled in another way. The government needed to invest in a policy of *in situ* development of the bastis, instead of the large-scale dislocation, disruption and displacement. The Left Front government in West Bengal did follow a policy of regularising the bastis in Calcutta, giving occupants rights and helping to develop the bastis. It built an alternative path, one that put the interests of the urban poor first, rejecting the policy that the only path to 'development' and 'beautification' is by making the poor invisible and banishing them to, or outside, the edges of the city. What such an inhuman policy also ignores is that the poor play a critical economic part in the life of the city by providing myriad essential services.

Women's Work

I had been working in workers' colonies during the Emergency. As mentioned earlier, I used to sleep over at Ramesh's house. There were two small rooms. Ramesh and Manju slept in one. Ramesh's mother Omvati, whom I called Amma, slept in the other, a corner of which had a kerosene stove and so doubled up as the kitchen. I shared this room with Amma. Across the courtyard from them lived Ramesh's brother, Suresh, with his family.

I would often have long conversations with Amma and Manju. They would also sometimes invite other women over for discussions. It is through these conversations and the experience of living with them that I learnt of the invisible burdens that women had to carry. The reproduction of labour power, which Marx talks about, would be impossible without the unending, unpaid, unrecognised, uncounted work that women did — but it took me some years to make this explicit theoretical connection. At the time, I was simply soaking it all in by listening to women from working-class homes and observing their hard lives. Prices were high, the public distribution system (the 'ration system') worked poorly, and workers' wages never kept up with the families' expenses. I noticed how Amma would divide food. She would serve her son first; the children would be fed next; Manju and she ate last — and sometimes least. The inequity in the intra-family distribution of food, scarce resources and commodities is now well-researched and extensively documented, but for me, whose plate was served how much food and when became a stark symbol of how patriarchy and capitalism intertwine to make the sacrifice of women of working-class families almost mandatory.

Even as there was a rising political consciousness among workers, particularly among cadres, the role of women in their own families remained an issue that rarely came up for discussion. I remember a meeting I attended in Kabir Nagar, next to Sawan Park. It was a meeting of a Party auxiliary group (AG) to be attended by handloom and unorganised sector workers. While drawing up the agenda for the meeting, I listed a discussion point about how we behave within our families. Unlike bourgeois parties, where anyone can walk into an office and become a member, in a communist party, a great deal of attention is paid to the recruitment process. The party forms AGs in which those individuals who work on the mass or class front and show promise in terms of their work among the people, their political consciousness, and their interest in learning about Marxism are invited. The AG holds regular classes and discussions. These are on the tenets of Marxism, on political questions, and on principles of party organisation. Typically, the AG process carries on for a year. This gives an opportunity to each AG member to carefully consider if they would like to become a member of the party and for the party to assess if the individual is ready as well. Even after the AG process, the individual is offered a candidate membership (CM) for a year, during which they attend meetings of the party unit ('branch committee'), take part in discussions, and express their opinions, but do not have the right to vote. After one year, the party again assesses the individual's work and ideological development and then offers them permanent member (PM) status. But becoming a PM doesn't mean getting a free pass — every year, each party unit conducts a 'renewal' process, where each member's work and political development is collectively assessed, and only after that is the membership renewed. Not only is this process rigorous and scrupulous, but it is also highly democratic since each party member gets an opportunity to assess their own and their comrades' work, to speak freely and frankly about problems, issues, and challenges they face, to seek and give clarifications or explanations, and so on. This process enables members to understand each other better while also being objective about each other's contributions.

In the Kabir Nagar meeting, I had listed the behaviour of comrades in the domestic sphere because women had complained to me about wife-beating and other forms of domestic violence. One of the workers, Nathu Singh, said, 'Comrade, you told us in the last meeting that we must deal with the barriers in our work. That is what I did. I beat up my wife because she was obstructing my work'. Nathu Singh was a tall and lanky handloom worker who liked to drink. I was aghast at his statement, but before I could react, there was uproar in the room. 'Don't you have any shame', one worker said. 'You don't deserve to hold the red flag', another shouted. Nathu Singh had to apologise and promise not to beat up his wife again.

Typically, domestic violence went hand in hand with alcohol. In posh colonies, violence against women within the family is often hushed up, and bruises are concealed with makeup and dark sunglasses to keep up the pretence of a civilised elite culture. In working-class basties, on the other hand, with their tiny houses all nestled together on narrow lanes, there are no secrets. If a man gets drunk and beats up his wife (or beats her up even without being drunk), everybody comes to know. I started holding meetings with women. These meetings started out as basically sessions to share experiences. Since it was only women in the room, everybody felt comfortable sharing their confidences. The meetings were unstructured and allowed for open and freewheeling discussion. Women felt safe, and they felt they were being listened to and that their voices mattered. These meetings were not as regular as I'd have liked, but I was happy to see that the women who came to the meetings, apart from sharing their own experiences, were interested in politics and discussed how the Emergency affected them. For example, they spoke about the fear they felt about the forced sterilisation campaign. Thus far, these colonies had been a solid support base for Indira Gandhi, but during the Emergency, discontent was growing.

The Emergency was the time of forced sterilisation (*nasbandi*) for the working class and the poor, conceived by Sanjay Gandhi. The stated rationale was the neo-Malthusian argument that India was poor because our population was high. In the late eighteenth century, Thomas Malthus, in his influential essay 'Principle of Population', had argued essentially, that when high population growth overtook food supplies, catastrophe would follow. He particularly criticised the working classes, holding that it was their propensity to produce more children which was responsible for their poverty.

Centuries later, the colonies in Delhi, where the poor lived, saw the brutal implementation of a policy inspired by this view. Many government benefits became linked to producing a certificate that you were sterilised. For example, the lieutenant governor, Krishan Chand, issued an order that said people would have to pay for what had till then been free medical services in government hospitals unless they produced a certificate that proved they had been sterilised. Government departments got 'quotas' — they had to somehow round up men and take them to the sterilisation camps to achieve the numbers allocated to them; otherwise, they would be punished. Government employees and officials would descend upon workers' colonies with lists of people to be sterilised. Those on the list would then be herded like cattle and taken to camps. It was a terrifying experience for the poor. Workers would take leave and disappear to their villages to avoid sterilisation. Many believed that sterilisation would result in impotency or loss of sexual drive. This was why many women preferred getting sterilised rather than having their husbands go under the knife. Forced sterilisation was a topic of discussion among women, and listening to them, it was clear to me that Indira Gandhi was losing support among a section — poor urban women — that had been a strong base for her.

Elsewhere in Delhi, there were courageous struggles led by

students and teachers, particularly in JNU. I would hear details of these from Prakash. Many SFI activists had gravitated towards the Party at the time. The president of the JNU Students' Union at the time was D.P. Tripathi (who became a prominent Nationalist Congress Party politician in later years). He was arrested soon after the Emergency was declared. Prabir Purkayastha, another student leader, was also arrested. The police sought to terrorise and silence students by conducting raids in the hostels and on campus in general. But the students were not cowed down. I heard of a dynamic and charismatic young woman called Ashoklata Jain, who became a prominent leader after Tripathi's arrest. She was a councillor in the students' union. The police tried to intimidate and hound her, but Ashoka, as she was fondly called, had steel in her spine. The students went on a strike under her leadership. Among those in JNU was Sitaram Yechury, a brilliant student who emerged as a popular leader of the SFI on campus. He went on to become the president of the Students' Union in the first election that was held after the Emergency. He led a students' march in September 1977 to Prime Minister Indira Gandhi's house. She came out to meet the protesters, and Sitaram read out a memorandum on behalf of the union with the demand that she resign as Chancellor of the university. This moment was captured in a striking photograph where you can see Sitaram reading the memorandum in front of Mrs Gandhi's house while she stands to the side, arms crossed, listening intently. This photograph keeps popping up periodically on social media.

I heard these stories from Prakash but never met any of these comrades at the time. They were in the thick of campus protests while I was busy working in the trade union organising workers. It was only after the Emergency was lifted that we came together and shared our experiences.

That time arrived sooner than any of us anticipated. On 18 January 1977, Indira Gandhi announced in a national broadcast on All-India Radio that elections were to be held in March.

Imprisoned leaders were released, and those underground could now move freely under their own names. It was a joyous time. Major Jaipal Singh, legendary leader of the Telangana armed uprising and secretary of the Party's Delhi state committee, arrived at the Party office to an ecstatic welcome by our supporters. Comrade Major had lived a life that would have been hard for an adventure novelist to cook up. A major in the colonial army, he organised a clandestine Council of Action within the force to help the freedom struggle. Under his leadership, the Council supplied arms to rebels during the 1942 Quit India Movement. Subsequently, in 1946, he uncovered a secret plot to assassinate nationalist leaders, including Nehru. He passed on this information to the socialists and communists. The British considered this treason. He deserted the army. Had he been caught then, he would surely have been court marshalled and shot. Despite having saved Nehru's life, the government of independent India arrested him in September 1947 and tried him for sedition in the infamous Fort William military jail. He pulled off a daring and improbable escape from this high-security prison. He then worked underground, training communist groups in different parts of the country in guerrilla warfare. He was arrested again in 1970 and spent a year in Alipore jail. His final jail term was during the Emergency, from June 1975 to November 1976. I was one amongst the throngs of people who had gathered at the Party's office in V.P. House on Rafi Marg in central Delhi to greet him. As I shook his hand and gave him a red salute, I knew that class struggle was going to take on a different hue.

III

POST-EMERGENCY

Euphoria and Hope

After the Emergency, 14 Vitthalbhai Patel House, Rafi Marg, the address of the Delhi State Committee of the CPI(M), became the hub of political activity. The Party secretary, Major Jaipal Singh, had a number of admirers across political parties. Leaders would drop in frequently, many of whom had been in jail with him. The main topic of discussion was the upcoming elections in March — would these be free and fair? Conspiracy theories swirled around. There was dark talk of intelligence agencies preparing lists for fresh arrests. Such theories gained credence because there were always one or two rather hapless characters, easily identifiable as intelligence agents, who would snoop around the Party office, eavesdropping on conversations.

But nothing could dampen the sense of euphoria and freedom that seemed ever-present — not just around the office but in the city as a whole. There was an unspoken bond among people. Strangers would smile at one another and exchange greetings as though they had collectively escaped a nightmare. In the DTC buses, which were earlier silent, there was loud talk and laughter. Every traveller had a political opinion, and no-one was willing anymore to keep it to themselves. Prakash and I still lived in Model Town, and I used to take bus number 100 to the Central Secretariat, a ten-minute walk from the Party office. The area was full of offices of the central government, and one would find groups of employees here and there, arguing and sharing the latest political gossip.

In February 1977, the prominent Congress leader Jagjivan Ram dropped a bombshell. He was not only a senior minister in Indira Gandhi's cabinet, but he was also probably the tallest Dalit leader in the party. Under his leadership, in defence of democracy, a group of Congress leaders left the party. This gave a real fillip to the opposition's efforts against the Congress. There was much talk of the need for the anti-Congress vote not to be split by ensuring one-on-one contests. All-in-unity against the Congress was the political flavour of the day.

The opposition announced a series of public meetings. The first of these was to be held at the historic Ramlila Maidan. Adjacent to the New Delhi Railway Station, this long and narrow ground is wedged between Old and New Delhi, with Turkman Gate and Delhi Stock Exchange on one side, and Delhi Gate and the erstwhile Irwin Hospital — to be rechristened Lok Nayak Jai Prakash Narayan soon, in November 1977 — on the other. It was here that Jai Prakash Narayan ('JP') had given that memorable speech on 25 June 1975, in which he called for 'total revolution', and quoted the poet Ramdhari Singh Dinkar:

Sinhasan khali karo ki janata aati hai
Vacate the throne, for the people are on the move

That same midnight, Indira Gandhi proclaimed the Emergency and all major opposition leaders, including JP, were arrested. That rally had been massive, with over 100,000 people spilling over far beyond the ground itself. We knew that this rally was also going to be huge, so Prakash and I made our way to Ramlila Maidan early, well before the announced time. It was early February, and I remember it was a cold evening, but we sat on the slightly damp ground, oblivious to the cold, chatting excitedly with people around us. All the major opposition leaders were there: Jagjivan Ram, Atal Bihari Vajpayee, Charan Singh, Morarji Desai, and Chandra Shekhar. Each of them received an enthusiastic and spontaneous ovation from the attentive crowd. It was exhilarating. I felt Jagjivan's Ram speech was the most impressive. He spoke slowly in a deep voice, weighing every word.

Prakash and I attended as many such public meetings as we could. I had never experienced such a palpable sense of hope and optimism, which seemed to pervade the very air we breathed. There was no doubt — the people were going to defeat the forces of the Emergency.

Speaking at the Gate

Back in north Delhi, the mill gates were once again transformed into bustling centres of activity, with hundreds of workers entering and exiting as one shift ended and the next began. Scores of tea shops lined the roads. At any given time, you would find several groups of workers standing around or squatting on the pavement, sipping tea and discussing politics. My favourite tea stall was the one run by Sardar Amar, who made the most delicious tea. You could order a badi chai or a chhoti chai (large tea and small tea), which he served in the appropriately sized cup. I remember those early winter mornings, misty and with a hint of damp in the air when I would stop at Sadar Amar's on the way to the morning shift gate meeting not only for the tea but also for the atmosphere that characterised working class Delhi — where political discussions and a sense of camaraderie pervaded the air.

Outside the gate, there used to be a row of large blackboards, between five to six feet tall, each belonging to a union. These blackboards were used to convey information to union members and the workers at large — a sort of news broadsheet. Every few days, the unions would write out their messages or news on their blackboard. A few days after the Emergency was lifted, the CITU sent a message to be written on the blackboards at all the five mills — something along the lines of, 'The people fought, the people won. The Emergency is gone, but the struggle remains'.

With this spirit, we plunged with renewed energy into union work. I spent countless hours at mill gates meeting workers, being introduced as a union activist. Public meetings at the mill gates — 'gate meeting', as they were called — had to be scheduled when workers went into the mill at the start of a shift. Naturally, two unions could not hold their meeting on the same day at the same time, so each union had to announce its meeting in advance, keeping in mind the schedule of other union meetings to avoid overlap. Despite the rivalry among unions, this system worked quite smoothly with mutual accommodation and cooperation.

Despite all the encouragement I received from comrades, I still did not have the confidence to address gate meetings. I was terribly self-conscious about my lack of fluency in spoken Hindi. To encourage me, comrades would cite examples of some of our tallest Party and trade union leaders, such as A.K. Gopalan from Kerala, amongst the founders of the CPI(M), or R. Umanath, former member of parliament from Tamil Nadu, neither of whom could manage any Hindi. They would address gate meetings in English, and although none of the workers really understood much of what they were saying, their tone and style still communicated a lot, and workers would invariably greet their speeches with loud applause!

The switch from the smaller and more secluded meetings during the Emergency to these large, almost daily gatherings of workers was an interesting transition for me. There is a special skill one must learn for gate meetings — how to speak precisely and make your points within a short, limited time. Workers would reach the gate around fifteen minutes before the shift was to begin and take time to settle down. Once the whistle blew, though, not even the best orator could retain the audience. They would all rush to enter the mill. I learnt this the hard way when once, in the middle of what I thought was a pretty decent attempt at public speaking in Hindi, the whistle blew and before you could've said Inquilab Zindabad, the area cleared, and not a soul was left, save the sympathetic tea sellers!

The first time I spoke at a gate meeting was when I was literally forced to by Comrade Ahilya Rangnekar. Ahilya was a member of Parliament, the first communist to win a Lok Sabha seat from Mumbai. She was immensely popular, and I soon learnt why. She

Rita speaking outside the Old Secretariat in Delhi in the early 1980s, at a demonstration agitating for demands of women workers.

had the ability to connect almost instantly with whoever she was speaking with — and she was always eager to know about those with whom she spoke. She rarely spoke about her own distinguished and highly inspiring life and had to be almost coerced into speaking about herself when AIDWA later brought out a publication called *Breaking Barriers* about the founders of the organisation. Ahilya was also a trade union leader, and we had asked her to address a gate meeting on the post-emergency struggle for the restoration of workers' rights.

We expected a good turnout and scheduled the meeting a good hour before the shift was to start, so it was not the usual hurried one. No sooner had she reached the gate when she quickly found out the list of speakers, and seeing that my name was not on it, she insisted that I be included. The comrade at the mic told her that I had declined to speak, but she refused to take no for an answer. She literally pushed me towards the mic, and much to my mortification, totally unprepared, I addressed my first meeting at the DCM gate. That was Ahilya — encouraging others to take the stage! I learnt from her and understood the importance of handholding, sometimes literally, to encourage young cadres to make public speeches, especially women who tend to be more self-conscious, particularly when surrounded by men.

At the time, I was a lone woman trade unionist among male workers and union organisers. The women workers earlier employed in the mills had been retrenched even before the Emergency. I don't recall any instance of sexism that I faced. The workers treated me just the same way that they treated male union organisers. I did have some nasty experiences with leaders of opposing unions, but that was when they sided openly with the management against the workers, and we called them out. Some of the older workers told me that the first woman unionist to work among Delhi's textile workers was the renowned freedom fighter, Aruna Asaf Ali. She was immensely popular among workers and later became mayor of Delhi. She was a pioneer, and I was grateful to her for having paved the way for young women like me. I now look back at the time and am rather amazed that the attitudes of the workers towards me were more open, equal, and democratic than some of my experiences decades later as a member of a male-dominated parliament.

Congress Faces Defeat

Immediately after Indira Gandhi's announcement in January 1977 that elections would take place in mid-March, the upcoming polls became the central preoccupation for everybody in the trade union movement. Our main aim was to ensure the defeat of the Congress and any other force that had supported the Emergency. In Delhi, the Party decided to support Janata Party candidates. Some of the localities where textile workers lived came under the sprawling East Delhi parliamentary constituency. The Janata Party candidate here was the former Congress leader Kishore Lal. Workers knew him well. He had been involved in the negotiations that had led to the nationalisation of the ATM. The Janata Party candidate from the Sadar Bazar constituency was Kanwar Lal Gupta, formerly of the Jan Sangh. He had been in the same barracks as Comrade Major in prison, and this certainly made him a wee bit more acceptable to our Party cadre, despite his Jan Sangh connection. We had decided that we would carry out an independent campaign under our own red flag rather than join the Janata Party campaign. Through our campaign, we wished to highlight the attacks on the working class and the poor, and project our charter of how to build a genuine alternative that would focus on policies rather than leaders. We also criticised the use of religion and religious symbols by some forces. In contrast to the Janata Party, whose campaign focussed almost exclusively on the restoration of democracy and civil liberties, our campaign was broad-based, encompassing civil rights, workers' rights, and secularism.

We would move around on tempos (open, small trucks) fitted with loudspeakers. A tempo can accommodate thirty-five to fifty people. As our tempo moved from spot to spot in workers' colonies, including the new resettlement colonies, we would address street corner meetings. I was happy that I was able to persuade a few women from workers' families to join the campaign. As one of us addressed the crowd, the rest would fan out, distributing leaflets. We also collected donations from the audience — small amounts, but since a number of people contributed, it was enough to cover our expenses. The response among the people was favourable, even enthusiastic. It was clear that the Congress was headed for a drubbing. And, as expected, when the results were declared a few days after the elections on 23 March, the Janata Party and its allies swept all the seven seats in Delhi. There was no doubt that the working-class colonies had contributed in a big way to this defeat of the Congress.

At the national level, the Janata Party won a handsome victory with 295 seats, the Congress was reduced to 154 (a loss of 198 compared to its previous tally), and the CPI(M) was the third largest party in parliament with 22 seats. Most of the Party's seats were from West Bengal. When our newly elected MPs arrived in Delhi, we went to the airport to greet them with red flags and slogans. The West Bengal results were truly inspiring — the Party had performed incredibly well despite the ferocious repression of the last five years when our comrades faced semi-fascist terror unleashed by the Congress government and goons. The Party had fought for the people, and the people had reposed their faith in the red flag. The Left Front won a huge victory in the assembly elections that were held later that year, the first of seven consecutive victories over thirty-five years. There was a special fragrance in the air — the fragrance of hope.

Reorganising our Work

Before we got married, Prakash and Amma stayed in V.P. House. The V.P. House is a hostel for members of parliament. Unlike in bourgeois parties, the accommodation allotted to MPs is often shared with Party wholetimers. For example, if an MP is allowed three separate rooms in the hostel, they may stay in one, and the other two may be allotted to wholetimers. Often, a bungalow allocated to a senior MP is parcelled out among several wholetimers, and the same bungalow may even have an office or two! Communist MPs are different from others. Approachable, with no airs, they are disciplined cadre, and are treated within the Party no different from others. Delhi is a city plagued by 'VIP culture', and communist MPs stand out for their humility and simplicity. In the 1970s, in particular, they saw themselves as ambassadors for the alternative culture of the Left.

Prakash was allotted a room in V.P. House before the Emergency, and we moved back there now. That single-room apartment was to be our home for the next thirty-seven years, from 1977 to 2014, the year our Party's seats in Parliament were reduced drastically.

My usual routine would include dropping into the Delhi Party office on the ground floor of V.P. House to chat a bit with Comrade Major before leaving for north Delhi. Often sharing the rather frayed sofa with him would be another veteran comrade, Shadi Ram, whom everyone affectionately called 'Chacha' (uncle). Born in a Dalit family, Chacha left his village in Haryana at a young age and joined the water department of the Delhi Municipal Corporation. For over two decades, Chacha had laid the pipes that supplied water to different parts of the expanding city. He

Rita with comrades of the Kapda Mazdoor Lal Jhanda Union. Chacha Shadi Ram (wearing turban) is to her right, and Inder Pal to his right. To Rita's left is Dayanand. Behind Rita (left to right) are Brij Bhushan, Avdesh Kumar and Chhote Lal. Sitting, second from right, is Tripurari.

took great pride in his work, and I would be fascinated listening to how he and his mostly Dalit co-workers faced the hazards of their job. He had long since retired but continued to be popular among municipal workers. He was elected president of the Delhi committee of CITU. Chacha was a wonderful, caring person, generous with his sagacious, down-to-earth advice. He was married to a tall, strapping woman who towered over him, whom we used to call Chachi. I shared a bond of great mutual affection with both of them. After one of our demonstrations had been water cannoned by the police, he took one look at me, bedraggled and drenched, and said, '*Rita tu bawli hai . . . Tu meri bawli beti hai*' ('Rita, you are crazy . . . My crazy daughter').

After the Emergency, my responsibilities included political work in the ATM and DCM areas. I was introduced to Dayanand, a worker from Bihar who had been dismissed from ATM for his union work, arrested during the Emergency, and got out on bail after a few months. I met him at the railway tracks along which the Azadpur jhuggis had proliferated. We walked along the track to the jhuggis where the workers lived. Dayanand also had a jhuggi here. He was very interested in learning more about theory and read as much as he could. He took classes on political developments and always had a class perspective in analysing current developments. Dayanand lived with his wife Geeta, who, when I first met her, was shy and always kept her head covered with her sari. I was a frequent visitor to their jhuggi, and she would feed me lunch. I can still remember the taste of that mouth-watering chutney she used to make. The food was simple but always delicious. Geeta, too, developed into an enthusiastic activist.

Dayanand introduced me to other comrades: Changur, Ram Naresh, Ram Preet, and Ram Dular. These were perhaps the most politically advanced workers in the union. They were from eastern Uttar Pradesh but couldn't afford to bring their families to Delhi since life in the metropolis was expensive. The camaraderie I saw between them was closer than among workers from other mills. Dayanand explained to me that they all belonged to Dalit or extremely backward communities and were mostly landless labourers. Maybe a few of them had tiny pieces of land, but their social and economic vulnerabilities as poor migrant workers were essentially the same. The cultural bonds among them were stronger than the 'local' workers.

I also got to know comrades in DCM. One was Nathu Parshad. He had been dismissed from the mill in 1970 for his union work and had become a wholetime union activist since then. He was imprisoned twice during the Emergency. He was a popular leader, young, dashing and militant. He lived with his wife and children in a small room in Manakpura, not far from the mill. He had beautiful handwriting, and he was the preferred choice for writing on the union blackboard. Nathu Parshad has been a lifelong communist and an important leader of our Party in Delhi, and I continue to be in touch with him. The other wholetime union activist in DCM was Babulal. He had the reputation of being a strongman who used to be on the side of the management earlier. When he came in touch with the CITU and saw what the union was doing for workers, he switched allegiances and became a staunch pro-union worker. He, too, was dismissed by the management for his union activities. His wife was as gentle as he was rough, and they lived in a small room in a lane called Ambalawali Gali.

Getting to the union gate for meetings at dawn used to be a challenge because few buses ran at that time, so I would stay overnight at either Nathu's or Babulal's — sometimes even unannounced. The grace and generosity of these and other comrades and their families towards me was as spontaneous as it was moving. The joke among the union leaders was that you always had to keep a sharp eye on Rita — there's no telling when she'll get pulled into a worker's home for a cup of tea or a meal, leaving the others high and dry and often hungry!

Lessons on Party Organisation

Once, PS was staying with Prakash and me in V.P. House. I used to leave very early every morning. He asked me the reason. I said I had gate meetings to attend. He sat me down and spoke sternly. 'You will become a victim of economism if you don't get your priorities right'. 'Economism' is the term Lenin used in his critique of trade unions that saw their role as only getting more benefits for the workers at the expense of developing the workers' political and class consciousness. Workers caught up in economism will never struggle to overthrow the capitalist system. 'You can address as many gate meetings as you wish, but it won't make any difference to the class struggle unless you prioritise introducing workers to socialist ideas and to the Party. That requires sustained, hard work and immense dedication', PS said to me.

He was right. The mill gate had become my addiction. I didn't feel my day was complete unless I visited one of the mill gates. After PS's admonition, I started focussing more on expanding the Party's presence among the working class. We formed AGs in the mill areas, in the larger industrial areas and even in resettlement colonies such as Jahangirpuri and Nand Nagri.

At the time, the political space in working-class areas was dominated by the Congress and, to a lesser extent, the CPI. It was a real struggle and challenge for us to create a base for the CPI(M). When the united CPI had split in 1964 in Delhi, the majority of the leadership had stayed with the CPI; only a handful came over to the CPI(M). As a result, the post-split CPI inherited the main Left base in working-class areas. The CPI(M) succeeded in building a base among college and university students and teachers. Comrades from DU played an important role in our efforts to expand in working-class areas by conducting political education classes for workers. Initially, the Jan Sangh (JS), the precursor to today's BJP, did not have much of a base among workers. After the elections of 1977, in which the number of Janata Party MPs from the erstwhile Jan Sangh totalled over 100, their influence grew. I started to notice more shakhas of the Rashtriya Swayamsevak Sangh (RSS) in workers' colonies. They would get together every morning in their khaki shorts and do their drill. The CPI(M) had been careful to maintain its own identity as distinct from the Janata Party, which was really an umbrella under which various anti-Congress parties had come together. I believed then and do so now that this was the correct approach. The Janata Party government, ushered in during an atmosphere of post-Emergency hope and euphoria, was no different from the Congress where issues of the working class were concerned. That the government and the ruling party also contained the toxicity of the RSS made matters worse.

Consequently, in the months following the formation of the Janata Party government, there was an explosion of struggles, agitations, gheraos, and strikes across India. Some observers felt that India was paying the price for its return to democracy with labour unrest. There were write-ups and editorials in the pro-business newspapers warning the government to curb industrial unrest. The new prime minister, Morarji Desai, had the reputation, not unfairly, of being pro-capitalist. Workers were not happy at his elevation. As Sohan Lal wrote on the DCM blackboard on the day of Morarji Desai assuming office, '*Billi rasta kaat gayi*' (literally, a cat has crossed one's way; idiomatically, an ill omen signifying that trouble lies ahead).

By the middle of May 1977, an estimated 200,000 workers in the organised sector were on strike in establishments, which included the Bombay port, the oil refinery in Baroda, some multinational firms such as Glaxo, and the bargemen of Calcutta. The Emergency is remembered now as a period that saw the suspension of democratic rights, gagging of the press, demolishing poor people's housing, and forced sterilisation. What people often forget is that it also represented a fierce attack on the working class and a cutting back of gains won by them. For example, the Bonus Act was amended by Indira Gandhi's government during the Emergency. This reduced statutory bonus to be paid to workers from 8.33 per cent to 4 per cent while granting those companies that declared no profits an exemption from having to pay bonus altogether. Government employees also had their demands, including the scrapping of the Compulsory Deposit Scheme (CDS). In the name of curbing inflation, government employees earning more than Rs 15,000 per month had to compulsorily deposit a certain percentage of their salary with the government. The Janata Party had promised that this money would be returned if it came to power. While the new government did reinstate thousands of railway workers who had been dismissed during the 1974 strike, it made no move to return the employees' money collected under CDS. In 1978, the government introduced the Industrial Relations Bill in parliament, which declared gheraos and go-slows — both legitimate tools of agitation used by workers — to be illegal and introduced provisions that made strikes much more difficult. The massive opposition by workers to the Bill ensured that the government felt it prudent to let it lapse rather than ram it through in parliament.

The restoration of democratic rights and civil liberties was a tangible victory. However, workers failed to see any change in the new government's economic or labour policy. In the industrial areas of north Delhi, in the G.T. Karnal Road industrial belt and Wazirpur, we knew of hundreds of industrial units that did not pay the government-stipulated minimum wage. Scores of workers from these areas started coming to the Kamala Nagar office requesting help to unionise so they could start getting the minimum wage. During 1977–78, we were able to form many CITU-affiliated unions. Although the legal right to unionise — suspended during the Emergency — had been restored, working conditions remained tough. Factory managements could dismiss workers with impunity. When this happened, the union would appeal, and the case would go in for 'labour conciliation'. This was and continues to be, a terribly unfair process for workers, tortuous and long drawn-out, and often workers would simply not have the economic ability to hold out. They would then be forced into what can only be described as distress resignations, accepting what in legalese would be called a 'full and final settlement' from the management.

The bourgeois notion of democracy in a capitalist society does not extend to workers' rights. We have to fight for a radical change in the labour policy of governments. Many of the leaders of bourgeois parties who fought the Emergency had no commitment to workers' rights. The system's bias against workers continued. The open and corrupt collaboration between labour inspectors and the managements of industrial units flourished as before. The bourgeois press and political parties refer to this derogatorily as 'inspector raj'. As a matter of fact, there was no inspector raj, since inspectors, many of whom had their pockets lined by managements, were most often simply absent on the ground. The government had no commitment to ensure the payment of minimum wage and other basic benefits. Through the unions, we organised numerous demonstrations at the Labour Commissioner's office. Many of these were successful and resulted in tangible benefits for the workers, while others were referred to the conciliation process.

This underlined the importance of PS's advice to me. Mere unionisation and fighting for economic gains were not going to bring about a change in the conditions of the working class. For that to happen, workers had to be brought into the political struggle to be encouraged to join the Party.

Strike Breakers' Ignominy

In August 1977, just before the festival of Raksha Bandhan, the Birla Mills management announced that it was declaring a holiday on that day, but would not give a holiday for Janmashtami. Raksha Bandhan is doubtless a popular festival in north India. There was a buzz in the workers' colonies because sisters would come to their brothers' houses to tie the rakhi, and brothers would give the sisters a gift, often cash, in return. Children would run around dressed in their best clothes, and much mithai would be had by everyone. Janmashtami, the birthday of Lord Krishna, was also a festive occasion with displays that recreated the birth of Krishna in captivity. Janmashtami was to fall in early September that year. While workers from other mills were getting a holiday that day, workers of Birla Mills had to report for work. The workers were naturally angry. The CITU-affiliated and the Congress-backed INTUC-affiliated unions decided to organise a strike, demanding that Janmashtami be declared a holiday.

I had spent the previous night at Ramesh's home and was participating in the picket at the labour gate. There was a substantial crowd of workers there in support of the strike. We were able to halt the morning shift at the gate itself, and the strike was successful. But we heard that some strike breakers had entered the mill from the officers' gate down the road. Before the shift was to end, I got an urgent message from Sriram to come to the officers' gate. I found Amma (Ramesh's mother Omvati) and Sheila (Sriram's wife) there. Amma was agitated. 'Our boys are giving up their wages for the general interest of all workers, and look at these officers and workers who have gone in to work. We must teach them a lesson today', she said. We knew that the strike breakers had to exit from this gate because the workers' gate was blocked by the picket. Little did they know that waiting for them were three furious women with the best antidote for strike breakers — a bucket of black paint and brushes.

The whistle blew. The shift had ended. Through the open gate, I saw that one of our members, Kripal, was also with the strike breakers. Seeing us, he knew trouble was afoot. He and the other strike breakers tried to rush through the gate, but we were agile and determined. The strike breakers had to face the ignominy of having their faces blackened. Kripal wasn't spared either. A largish crowd of workers had gathered, cheering us on. It was quite a scene. The management called the police, who conducted a mild lathi charge to disperse the crowd. The three of us were surrounded, forced into a van, and taken to the police station.

But the point had been made. The workers were in high spirits. The management, sensing the mood of the workers, agreed not to cut the day's wage. Amma, Sheila, and I were produced before the magistrate. I expected them to jail us, but he granted us bail. We returned as minor heroines. The story of how strike breakers had their faces blackened by three intrepid women spread to other mills, no doubt embellished in imaginative ways in every telling by the workers. A few days later, a shamefaced Kripal made an appearance at the union office. He gave a written apology and promised never to betray the workers again. This saved his union membership, but honestly, the workers never quite trusted him again.

Dirty Tricks Department

As the managements of the various mills increased the workloads of workers, spontaneous protest actions by workers in various departments also went up. More and more workers were open and receptive to our message of protest and struggle. We realised there was a great potential for us to expand our base. I guess the managements of the mills understood this, too, because we soon started sensing that they were trying the old trick of bribing union leaders. It was shocking for me that within our own union, too, the attitude of some of our important leaders started changing. We started getting reports that this or that union leader of the CITU was negotiating directly with the management, without discussing with or consulting any other office bearers, let alone the workers. This happened mainly in Birla Mills but also one or two of the state CITU leaders who were also helping our union in the textile industry. They would be seen in the company of the management's men or were calling them home for negotiations rather than in the union office. In some cases, the management would chargesheet some particularly militant CITU workers and the leader, instead of organising protests, would urge caution in the name of preventing further victimization. In this way, several mill-based union activists were victimised. This collaborationist trend was not limited to textile mills either; other sectors were also reporting similar stories. The state leadership of the Party and the trade union centre was aware of all this. At their level, they made attempts to speak to the concerned leaders, warning them of disciplinary action. But matters did not improve.

By 1978, we found our work getting affected. The atmosphere in the organisation changed. Instead of concentrating on building and expanding our base, for which the conditions were ripe, we were forced into a firefighting mode. Because of the pro-management approach of some leaders, our own membership in the union was getting divided rather than united. Other unions, alarmed at the growth of CITU, were glad that there was a division in the ranks. They started a vicious campaign against some of us. The management's hand would be clearly visible behind such attempts. One day at the DCM gate, I saw an unusual crowd gathered around the blackboard of one of the unions. Someone had written a nasty message on it, to the effect that CITU had brought 'a young woman' to distract the workers and thereby increase membership. My comrades from the CITU union were livid. They threatened to smash the board and got into a heated argument with members of the other union. The security guards intimidated CITU members and reported them to the management — clearly, this was the intention all along. The message remained on the board all day and led to sharp discussion and arguments among workers. It was all quite unpleasant for me, but the overall mood among the workers was against such low tactics, and I heard that those responsible for this were castigated by the workers.

A month or so later, the DCM management began discussions with the unions about the payment of bonus. The management had cut the bonus from 8.33 per cent to 4 per cent. The Janata Party government had made some alterations in the existing law that pegged the bonus to 8.33 per cent but had also left loopholes that the management could use to their advantage. All the unions came together and gave a joint call for a strike. We conducted a vigorous campaign of gate meetings before and after every shift. As the momentum picked up, the unions decided to take the campaign to other mills as well. We shared the responsibilities of going to different mills. I had to go to Birla Mills for the night shift meeting. The list of speakers who were to address meetings was jointly sent to all the gates by the united platform of unions, so it was public knowledge that I would be speaking at the Birla

Mills gate at night. We had been facing some problems in our union at the Birla Mills, which was on the verge of a vertical split, with many of the important leaders ranged against the CITU. A favourite phrase to describe collaboration with the management against worker interests was that 'the leader has a setting with the management'. This is what was happening in Birla Mills.

I reached the gate accompanied by a few comrades. A big crowd of workers had gathered for the meeting. I was explaining the importance of the fight for bonus and the principle of bonus as 'deferred wage' — in other words, to see bonus as something the workers had legitimately earned, not as the management's largesse — when suddenly the lights went out. It was dark; I could barely see anything; the mic had stopped working. In the confusion around me, I heard shouts of 'catch her'. Ramesh grabbed my arm, bent my head low, and pulled me away. 'Move fast, don't say a word', he said. We ran through some of the small lanes in Kamala Nagar, caught an autorickshaw, and he dropped me back to the DCM Mills gate. Ramesh and I were in a state of shock and couldn't fathom what had happened. We learnt that the strike in DCM had already started, so I decided to stay on at the DCM gate among our comrades. Ramesh went back to Birla Mills to get some information. He came back later at night and told me that I had been the target of a plan hatched by the manager of the mill, who he named, along with some other union leaders. They wanted me out of the area. This was subsequently confirmed to me by a Congress-connected union leader, Saudan Singh, who, even decades later, stays in contact with me. He said that the plan had been to humiliate me by stripping me and to blame this on 'angry' workers who were supposedly being forced to go on strike against their wishes. The switchboard for the gate lights was in the security guards' room. They had been given instructions by the manager to plunge the area into darkness when I started speaking. I spent the rest of the night with the striking workers at the DCM gate. Two days later, I was part of the team which negotiated the settlement for the three mills of the DCM group. All of them got the statutory bonus of 8.33 per cent. ATM, a nationalised mill, had already been given an 8.33 per cent bonus. Only in Birla Mills did the management succeed in disrupting the strike, and the workers didn't get the statutory bonus at the time, though later, they did come to some agreement. This was a huge learning experience for me.

Lessons Learnt

Capitalists and ruling class parties use many dirty tricks to break the unity of workers — they use physical violence and force; they lure with money; they sow divisions based on community, caste, language, and region. Management of factories break strikes and cripple militant unions using whatever tactic is handy at the time. This is not to say that there aren't differences among unions. What is usually christened 'inter-union rivalry' is often a reflection of a deeper conflict between two lines — that of struggle, and that of surrender and betrayal of workers' interests. Sometimes, these occur within one's own union, as happened with the textile workers union. By 1979, the split was official, and two unions started functioning with the same name, the difference being that the breakaway group lost its affiliation with CITU. Our union had the majority of the membership, although it did deplete our strength, thus helping the management.

When faced with the dirty tricks department, it is essential to remain calm, to not take hasty decisions, and not to give in to emotions or subjective assessments. Such decisions can prove immensely costly and damaging. In the case of Birla Mills, we had been weakened by the division in our own ranks. We had failed to correctly assess the lengths to which the management and its agents would go to break the workers' unity. Personally, I had been lucky that day — Ramesh sensed the danger instantly and moved quickly to rescue me. But the problem was larger. I had been considered a 'soft' target to demoralise the union. We held a meeting of the Birla Mills unit soon after this incident. At this meeting, our comrades shared what they had learnt of the conspiracy. They also identified the ringleaders. We decided to hold a gate meeting, which I addressed along with other leaders of the union. This time, we were well prepared, and there was even a team from ATM to bolster our presence. We had decided not to refer to the incident itself but to emphasise the need for the unity of workers, without which neither the demand for the bonus nor, indeed, any other demand could be won. I learnt an important lesson — never do anything that would indicate to the management that their tactics to weaken the union or the leaders have succeeded, even if partially. In a word, not an inch back! Not only did we go back to the gate and hold a large and successful meeting, but we also neither mentioned the attack nor did we criticise the other unions for being hand in glove with the management. The management and other unions' plans were punctured.

I also drew a more personal lesson from all this. I realised that when you stand firmly on class issues, personal relationships and friendships can get affected. Many comrades I had worked closely with, mainly from the Birla Mills unit, including Sriram and a couple from the DCM unit, became open critics of the CITU and did everything possible to weaken our union. Babulal had joined them, too. Once, when I passed his home, his wife was sitting outside, and I stopped to greet her. She knew what had happened and expressed regret that we could not meet like the old times. I did indeed feel sad, as I had quite close relationships with several of those who left with Sriram. I also realised how vulnerable women in political work can be. It is so much easier to humiliate a woman through sexist abuse and actions. I was fortunate to have escaped unscathed, but it taught me to be more mindful of people and circumstances around me. The union was reorganised, and a new leadership was elected. I continued as one of the secretaries of the union. I was also elected as the secretary of the north local committee of the CPI(M), which added to my responsibilities.

The Jalandhar Congress

In the midst of all this, there were significant developments taking place within the Party at the national level. There were lessons to be learnt for the Party from the experience of the Emergency. A Party Congress was held in April 1978, later famous as the Jalandhar Congress, named after the Punjab city in which it was held.

Communist parties don't work like bourgeois parties, where a single leader, a family, or a ruling cabal can more or less decide for the party as a whole. A communist party works on highly democratic principles. We hold a Congress once every three years. The Congress is the highest decision-making body in the Party. Delegates and observers are elected from every state who, in turn, elect the Central Committee (CC). The Polit Bureau (PB) and the General Secretary (GS) are then elected by the CC from among its members. The CC meets every quarter, and the PB, elected from among the CC members, is tasked with taking decisions between CC meetings. As a lead-up to the Party Congress, conferences are held at every level of the Party — from the individual unit all the way up to the State Committees. The draft Political Resolution of the Party Congress — the main political document that analyses the developments of the previous three years and sets out the strategic vision of the Party for the next three years — is circulated well in advance, and is discussed in great detail at all levels of the Party. The Party Congress receives literally thousands of amendments before and during the Congress — in a dozen or more languages, I should add. Each of these is read by the leadership, and the GS presents a report on the amendments at the Congress, explaining which amendments are accepted and which are not. It is only after this massive democratic exercise over about six months that the Political Resolution is finally adopted at the Congress.

I was elected as an 'observer' to the Congress. Observers don't have the right to vote or to speak but can listen to all the discussions. It was an inspiring experience for me. Having joined the Party as an auxiliary group member in Calcutta, then earning my full membership, working from the unit level, being promoted as a local committee member, being elected to the state committee, and now to be present at the first post-Emergency Congress, was such an honour. I was able to listen to the presentations of the top leadership of the Party and the lively debates that followed. These debates were the exact opposite of the caricature view of the communist party. Every delegate has the right to express her opinion — either through their state delegation or if they feel their viewpoint has not been adequately expressed, in writing. There is no other party in India which adopts such a democratic process.

The main political discussion at Jalandhar centred around the possibilities that had opened up in the post-Emergency situation. The CPI(M) had been in the forefront of the struggle against the Emergency. The role of communist cadre had been noted and appreciated by a large section of people. How to reach out to them, how to build our independent base even while keeping intact the unity achieved by the anti-Emergency forces were some of the questions before the Party Congress. Despite the divide over the draft report, the congress concluded with the Party united in a resolve to develop the party across the country through strengthening its links with the people. We stood up to collectively sing the *Internationale*, led by the West Bengal contingent.

After Jalandhar

I came back determined to help build the Party among the textile workers in my adopted political home, north Delhi. In 1979, a joint platform of textile unions was formed to take up the issues of wage revision and the long-standing demand for the implementation of the Vaidyalingam Award. This award had recommended a 90 per cent dearness allowance calculated on the basis of the inflation index, but the mill owners, by manipulating the method of counting workdays, in effect gave a DA of 78 per cent, thus saving a full 12 per cent. At the time, the basic wage of a textile worker was a mere thirty rupees per month. Many departments in the mills had implemented a system of productivity-linked wages. In the weaving department, for example, a worker's wage was directly dependent on how many metres of cloth he wove. This was one of the ways in which the management squeezed every drop of productivity from the workers, often with deleterious effects on their health.

Then there was the issue of the so-called 'helpers' and 'badli' workers. These workers did exactly the same work as the permanent or *jatu* workers, but received only the basic wage with no allowances. In addition to the work they were contracted to do, they were also tasked with other tasks, often considered 'menial' — cleaning the floor or the machines or working the looms. Chhote Lal, one of the 'helpers' in the weaving department at Swatantra Bharat Mills, described his work to me as being in a snowstorm, only 'it's not snow but cotton fluff that you breathe in', and that it 'sticks everywhere — on your clothes, on the floor, on the machines. And we have to clean all of it'. Helpers and badli workers received as wage approximately half of what jatu workers received, which was low to begin with in any case. As prices rose, the real wages of workers shrank further.

Workers started forming *khata* or floor-level committees to articulate their dissatisfaction. Many militant demonstrations were held at the gates, in front of the labour offices, and so on. We began a campaign among workers' families to gather wider support. Two young women played a stellar role in helping reach workers' families. Ashalata was the daughter of Adi Narayan, a leader of the Postal Workers' Union, and Ujjwal was the daughter of Pramila and M.K. Pandhe, both veteran leaders of the working class. Ashalata and Ujjwala would visit the area regularly and interact with the families of the workers. As a result of their efforts, women from working-class families also started joining the demonstrations. In subsequent years, Ashalata became an important leader of the women's movement in Delhi.

As the workers' anger became increasingly manifest, even the most pro-management unions had to join the struggle. It was around this time that Lalit Maken emerged as a major figure in Delhi politics. He was a young Congress politician who was a metropolitan councillor and had a following in the unions and among workers. He threw in his lot with the workers. (Lalit Maken was subsequently elected to the Lok Sabha. Soon after that, however, he was assassinated by Sikh extremists for his alleged role in the murder of Sikhs in the wake of Indira Gandhi's assassination. He was 34. His wife, who also died in this attack, was the daughter of Shankar Dayal Sharma, who later became President of India.)

The joint platform of unions made every effort to start negotiations on the workers' demands in order to avoid a strike. Members of parliament also approached the government to intervene and sort out the issues. But the Janata government was unsympathetic. It was rapidly losing support among workers.

There was a big public meeting in a ground near the DCM Mills attended by thousands of workers. We requested B.T. Ranadive (or BTR, as he was affectionately called), Polit Bureau member of the CPI(M) and founder-president of CITU, to speak on behalf of our union. BTR, one of the foremost leaders of the working class in India and a veteran of many a struggle, would always counsel us on fighting the dominant trend among the unions, that of unprincipled compromise with the anti-labour steps of the managements. At the public meeting, BTR gave a sharp speech in which he exposed the class character of the Janata government, even as he demarcated it from the previous Congress regime. Other leaders, many of whom had a national stature, whitewashed the role of the Janata government. BTR later called me to castigate us. 'What kind of struggle are you building? Volunteers are all ours, and the leaders theirs? This will only weaken the struggle.' It was true. Apart from BTR himself, we didn't have any other leader from CITU addressing the workers, while others had several national leaders. BTR was always clear about this. United struggles of workers must result in the strengthening of the revolutionary line. Dominance by reformist leaders, particularly when our cadre did so much of the groundwork, weakened the struggle. He was critical that in the name of unity, we often shied away from sharply articulating our politics among workers.

The 1979 Strike

The strike started on June 27, 1979. When a strike began, hundreds of workers would congregate at the mill gate, no matter what the time of day or night it was. We would move from one centre to another, holding meetings and planning actions. Being on strike is not a holiday. It is hard work, and if the strike continued beyond a few days, it meant severe economic hardship. A week or two into the strike, we organised community kitchens and distributed meals. Groups of workers would collect funds and relief for the strikers. The management would retaliate by issuing chargesheets and dismissal notices to the leaders of the khata committees.

One day, a peon from Birla Mills went to the mill quarters where Harish Chandra Pant — hero of the 1976 strike — lived with his and his brother's family to deliver a letter from the management. Pant's family was in economic distress. Just two months before, Pant and his wife Basanti Devi had celebrated the birth of their second son. The birth of a child is a joyous occasion, but it also means increased expenditure. Once the strike began, they had to cut down on their food. All they could afford was rotis cut into small bits mixed with cheap cooking oil and salt. The peon handed over the letter to Basanti and told her that her husband had been 'dismissed'. She had no idea what this English word meant. She repeated the word to Pant and asked him innocently, 'Does this mean something good?' Pant had no option but to send his family back to Uttarakhand (then UP). Even all these years later, that image is imprinted on Pant's brain — his wife looking at him from the moving bus, tears streaming down her face, clutching the infant in her arms while the elder waved to Pant, his little face glued to the window.

Such scenes became more frequent as the strike entered its second month. It was particularly hard on the women, who had to somehow keep the family expenses balanced. Many women started working. When we went to the workers' living quarters, we found that many women had started doing home-based work. I remember going to a meeting organised by Bishen Pal, a leader in the DCM Mill, in the lane where he lived. The women spoke about the difficulties they were facing and the need to find work. Bishen Pal's wife Asha, along with their children, was cutting small pieces of copper wire from a large bundle and winding it on an iron screw. They worked all day and somehow managed to make forty rupees a day on average. This somehow helped the family survive. The thing about home-based work is that, inevitably, the entire family ends up doing it. It eats up the family's entire time. Children start missing school, and some even drop out — all this to somehow help the family survive. Some women found work as domestic helpers.

What was striking, though, was the spirit of the women and their resolve to see the strike through. Symbolic of this spirit was Kamla, wife of Inder Pal, one of our leaders in Swatantra Bharat Mills, who later became general secretary of the union. She was shy and had an air of preoccupation about her, no doubt a result of looking after the needs of the joint family. She agreed to our request to join the campaign among the workers' families in support of the strike. She had a grace and dignity that made an immediate impact with her words. She spoke about the difficulties she faced as a mother of four school-going children, of the way that she had to divide what food they had among the family, she spoke about workers' dignity and pride, and about how much hard work they put in. She roused anger against injustice — it was a moving experience to hear her speak.

Some people think unions love to have workers go on strike. Capitalist media helps propagate such lies. In fact, workers hate strikes more than anyone. Strikes are literally their last resort. Living on subsistence wages, as the textile workers did, they had no savings to tide them through a no-wage strike period. They knew a strike would drive them into debt, and indeed, hundreds of workers did go into debt. The support of families for striking workers is crucial. It affects their morale deeply. In that sense, working-class families are also a centre of the struggle against capitalist exploitation.

Most unions do not bother about the women in the family. In a state like West Bengal, where the Party had grown in the colonies where workers lived, women of working-class families were involved in the politics of class struggle. I remember when I was working in Calcutta, I went for a brief period to the workers' colonies around the Khidirpur dock area. The leader of the union, a wise and gentle worker originally from Bihar called Babu Nandan, told me that one of the greatest strengths of strike struggles is the support from a worker's family. He said it was the Party's work which built support for the struggle in the residential areas around the dock in Calcutta.

In Delhi, where the Party had a limited reach, there were no such support groups. In a small way, our band of women volunteers had taken the issues of the strike to the workers' families. We found that there were hardly any family discussions on the issues of the strike. Clearly, patriarchal cultures prevailed in workers' families, too, where issues linked to work, unions, and struggles were not part of family interactions, leave aside discussions. We started inviting women to the workers' meetings. Not many would come, but word got around that such meetings were being held. At the gate meetings, we urged workers to discuss the issues of the strike at home with their wives and children. One of our slogans tried to sharpen this point:

Sangharsh hamara —
Gate se ghar tak,
Ghar se gate tak!
Our struggle —
From the gate to the home,
From the home to the gate!

It was a good beginning, but the economic pressures were such that more and more workers left with their families to go back to their villages.

Prison

I often hear it being said that workers' issues should not be politicised. This is utter humbug. If the government's pro-capitalist bias is not 'political', then what is? Many solidarity actions were organised by the central trade unions, supported by Left parties. There was a march to parliament demanding government intervention. Apparently, when MPs raised the issue with Prime Minister Morarji Desai, he said, 'When their [flour] canisters are empty, workers will themselves go back to work'. As chief minister of the erstwhile Bombay State, Morarji Desai had pursued an aggressively pro-capitalist, anti-worker policy. Now Delhi's workers could appreciate why he was resented so much by their Bombay brethren.

Sometime at the end of July 1979, a call was given for a general strike in solidarity with textile workers. I was in a large demonstration along with workers from the industrial areas. We were crossing Kamala Nagar when we were confronted by a large police force that blocked our path. Without warning, they started a lathi charge, to which the workers retaliated. The inspector leading the charge was from the Roshanara Road police station. He grabbed my arm, beat me on the head, and began dragging me to the police van. When I resisted, he began pulling my hair. I slapped him hard and was beaten again. Dayanand was by my side, along with another worker, Ganesh. They tried to protect me, and they, too, were badly beaten. The police lathi-charged workers at other sites as well, and 83 workers from different unions were arrested that day. We were presented before a magistrate, who sent us off to Tihar jail.

We were all taken in the same vans, but I, the only woman, was separated from the rest once we got to the jail. I was a bit apprehensive as to what lay ahead since I had heard many stories of the conditions that prisoners had to face during the Emergency. I was taken to a medium-sized room, which didn't at all appear like a prison cell except for the bars on the windows. There was a cot with clean bedding placed on it, a table, and a chair. There was also a toilet — quite clean — shared by a limited number of inmates. I was astounded. The warden saw my reaction and informed me that I was in the same cell that Indira Gandhi had been in when she was arrested the previous December! I had no idea why I was brought here instead of the normal cells, but as a result, my first stint in jail was not what I had imagined it would be. All my subsequent jail stays, however, have been in small and cramped cells where one had to sleep on the floor and share dirty toilets. Jail reform is still an urgent agenda, especially now under the present regime where prisoners locked up on political grounds are denied even the most basic amenities.

I met some of the other inmates when we were allowed to move around outside the cells. Among them was a young Australian woman called Mary Ellen. We would meet almost every day, even if for a short while. I was fascinated by her stories. She was involved in the Charles Sobhraj serial killing case and claimed that she had been trapped and cheated. Later, I heard that she had turned approver and got an early release from jail. One day, when I was called to the superintendent's office to meet my lawyers, I found the room occupied. It was Charles Sobhraj. He was sitting on a corner bench with a woman, also a co-accused in the case, holding her in a close embrace — an unusual scene in the Jail Superintendent's office!

Most of the workers were released in a few days, but along with a few others, I had been charged with attempt to murder under Section 307, in addition to the bailable sections. The inspector who had attacked me had filed a complaint that I, along with some others, had tried to murder him! It was later struck down by the court, but it was three weeks before we got bail. We came back to a warm welcome by workers at the gate, but the situation was grim.

The Agreement

The Janata Party was caught up in its inner contradictions and rivalries, and finally, in July 1979, the government collapsed. Charan Singh formed a new government. Even before he could face parliament to prove his majority, though, the Congress, which had initially supported his bid for prime ministership, withdrew its support. On 22 August 1979, the Lok Sabha was dissolved. Charan Singh's government was declared a 'caretaker' government till the next Lok Sabha elections, which were held in January 1980.

When such unexpected political developments take place, it is the macro picture that people are interested in. But for us, during an already prolonged strike, it was disastrous. The mood amongst the workers was one of depression and demoralisation. We had little hope that the government would do anything to help. But surprisingly, the new government, with Fazal-ur-Rehman as the Labour Minister, did call the workers and all the unions for talks. We sent a team of office bearers, one representative from each mill, led by the new general secretary, ('doctor') Kamal Narayan. Every day after the negotiations, we would meet at the home of veteran CITU leader M.K. Pandhe. He had a wealth of experience in negotiations and gave the team advice.

We also convened meetings of workers to keep them informed. Once the negotiations commenced, the gates were once again crowded with workers eager to know the latest news. There were two main issues. The first was to raise the percentage of dearness allowance. The second was to ensure no victimisation and the withdrawal of all dismissal notices. The other demands, such as reference to a tribunal for wage increase, had already been decided. The eventual agreement once again referred the implementation

116

issue of the amount of the dearness allowance to yet another committee — the only positive here was that it was a time-bound reference, and later, the dearness allowance was, in fact, increased to the correct interpretation of 90 per cent. The managements had to accept the demand for no victimisation, and had to withdraw all punitive measures. There were differences among the unions on a clause related to productivity norms, which the managements insisted on. The government supported the management. Most of the unions agreed to refer the productivity norm issue to a tribunal whose orders would be final and binding.

We were strongly opposed to this. It was not that workers were shirking their work responsibilities, but the managements had refused to make any new investments while burdening the workers with a heavier load. We suggested that there could be a separate discussion on this between the managements and the workers once the strike was lifted. Our main concern was the retrenchment of workers. While we agreed with the other clauses, we did not sign the productivity clause. If the unions had remained united, we could have got this through. But once again, the reformist unions buckled under pressure. It would prove costly in the days to come, but at that time, the workers were relieved that an agreement had been arrived at. The strike had gone on for almost four months.

The political fallout was a dramatic change in the mood of the workers in support of the Congress. In the 1980 Lok Sabha elections following the collapse of the Janata Party government, except for the seat won by Atal Bihari Vajpayee, the Congress won six of the seven seats in Delhi. The terrific performance of the Left parties, winning 47 seats (37 for CPI(M) and 10 for CPI), primarily from West Bengal and Kerala, was a big boost for the alternative politics which we were trying to project. The higher profile of the Left gave us a boost in Delhi, too. It helped the party expand its base to newer areas.

Working Women's Convention, 1979

In the aftermath of the strike, the membership of the union increased, as did our contacts in various residential colonies. We developed new cadre and brought them into the Party. This played a direct role in helping us build organisations of women and youth the following year. The local committee of the Party was expanded to include student representatives, one among whom was Subodh Varma from St. Stephen's College, DU. A highly committed and articulate young man, he developed as a trade union leader of the area and a state committee member of the Party. We won seats in the Mill Working Committees. Some of the leaders of the strike were among those elected.

There was an important development in 1979. The CITU national centre decided that more importance had to be given to bringing working women into the trade unions and enhancing their role. CITU decided to form a Coordination Committee of Working Women. This initiative came from B.T. Ranadive, who famously said, 'When Marx said, "*Workers of the world unite*", he was not referring to just the male working class!'

In January 1979, along with Ranjana Nirula, I was given the responsibility to organise the first working women's convention of CITU in Delhi, which had to be held before April when the national convention was scheduled. Ranjana had joined the Left movement in Delhi in the early seventies on her return from the United States, where, as a student, she had been influenced by the movement against the imperialist war on Vietnam. She joined the Party soon after the Emergency and shifted to Faridabad in 1978, where she lived in workers' colonies and worked with CITU unions. She was a wonderful comrade and friend. She did pioneering work organising first-generation women workers in the emerging industrial areas of the region.

Between us, we worked out that it was more practical to hold the convention in north Delhi, which would be accessible to the working women we hoped would participate. There were many other women activists like Babli Gupta and Nina Rao who were involved in organising the convention. Students from JNU also helped. We did a quick survey of 500 or so women, helped by CITU workers. Some of the issues of importance which emerged included equal wages, better transport facilities, identity cards for domestic workers, fixed rates for handloom women workers, and creches. In Faridabad, Ranjana had come across examples where young women workers had to get permission from male supervisors to use the toilet and were subjected to humiliation and sexual innuendos constituting sexual harassment. We included demands for the protection of women in the workplace, perhaps one of the earliest demand charters of working women, which included sexual harassment at the workplace after the Emergency. It was a new dimension of trade union work.

During our preparation, a young theatre activist who was with Jana Natya Manch (Janam), an energetic and talented street theatre group with a strong pro-worker left orientation, contacted me. This was the charismatic and gifted Safdar Hashmi, who a decade later was martyred while performing a play for the CITU in Jhandapur, Sahibabad, on the outskirts of Delhi — brutally murdered by Congress goons. He suggested that Janam do a play on working women, which they would perform at the convention. We had a long discussion, and I shared my experiences of the lives of working-class women and the combination of capitalism and patriarchal notions on their lives. He listened keenly and brought new dimensions to the discussion. For example, he wanted to know how a strike might impact the education of a girl child in a working-class family or whether dowry affected workers' families too. I also met Moloyashree Roy, the brilliant actor and Janam member, then about twenty-five years old, who played the main protagonist in the play. She and Safdar got married later that same year, in 1979. The play that Janam produced was called *Aurat*. This play, barely 25 minutes long, was a powerful depiction of the inequalities and humiliations that women face in various roles and situations — as a girl child, as a middle-class educated woman, and as a working-class woman. Moloyashree's performance in particular, was memorable — searing, scintillating, and inspiring in equal measure. *Aurat* would surely be counted as one of the best-ever plays in the history of street theatre in India. I'm proud that it was created for, and first performed at, the Working Women's Convention held in a hall in Roop Nagar in north Delhi in March 1979.

Documents of the convention record that it was attended by 192 women. The largest contingent was of handloom workers, followed by those working in factories organised by the Delhi-based General Mazdoor Lal Jhanda Union. There were domestic workers, individual women in the unorganised sector, and fifteen women workers from Faridabad. There were also schoolteachers as well as teachers from DU. This was the first women's convention that I was involved in organising, and I remember how nervous I was that morning. Although we had worked hard to mobilise women, we weren't sure how many would actually come. The lives of working-class women are so precarious, and they juggle so many responsibilities that their time is not always their own. Their plans often change, determined by factors beyond their control. But that day, the women came, and around thirty of them spoke, each making a public speech for the first time in their lives. One of them, whom we had met during our survey in Nand Nagri, said that she felt as though a block in her mind, her heart, her voice, had suddenly been removed, and the words just came rushing out. She was a widow, a stone breaker, employed by various contractors doing road work in resettlement colonies. The pride and joy I felt that day is etched in my memory.

Moloyashree and other Janam actors during the first performance of *Aurat* in March 1979 at the Working Women's Convention in Roop Nagar, Delhi.

The convention was inaugurated by Vimal Ranadive, a freedom fighter and devoted communist who had earlier been involved with the organisation of women tea garden workers in West Bengal. A month later, she became the founding national convenor of the Working Women's Coordination Committee (WWCC), formed at the third conference of the CITU in April 1979. Although I was the WWCC convenor in Delhi, I was unable to attend the first conference of the Working Women's Coordination Committee because of my work with the textile union and preoccupation with struggles in Delhi. Seven working women delegates attended the conference from Delhi. Vimal Ranadive, in her youth, had been an actor in a few films, but inspired by the freedom struggle, she soon gave up her fledgling career. She later married B.T. Ranadive, and together, they made immense sacrifices for the revolution. Vimal Ranadive was also a founding leader of AIDWA. Along with her sister-in-law Ahilya, Vimal had been among the women delegates in Jalandhar who had raised the issue of building a national women's organisation.

The cooperation between different sections of the movement, such as the talented Janam artists, JNU students, DU teachers and students, and the trade unions, was one of the key factors in the efforts to mobilise working women. This experience was also important for us when we began building organisations of women and youth the following year and sought to develop the Left movement in the politically barren landscape of Delhi.

Building the Party

I was amid multiple tasks: at the grassroots level as a union organiser, at the political level as the secretary of the north local committee of the Party, and now with the responsibility to work towards building a women's organisation in Delhi. Unlike in the states where the Party has a wider base and more cadre, in states like Delhi, most of the state committee members had to take on multiple responsibilities. The Kamala Nagar office was now bustling with the work of the expanded trade unions in the industrial areas. There was little space for political work, Party meetings, or discussions. We ran a fund collection campaign to build a separate office for the Party local committee.

We had a discussion on who could take on the responsibility of actually overseeing the building of the office, and the ATM unit suggested the name of Shanti, a woman who lived in the jhuggis around the mill. She was an independent and feisty woman with her signature white saree. Once, I asked her why she insisted on wearing white. Her answer reflects a common experience that many single women face who develop strategies to protect themselves. She explained that after she had been widowed at a young age and had decided not to get married again, she found she was the target of unwanted attention, bordering on sexual harassment. She said, 'I thought if I could wear white and emphasise my identity as a widow in perpetual mourning, I could escape the fate of sexual harassment from the men I have to deal with'.

Shanti became a member of the Party and took her responsibilities seriously. She built the modest office in record time. It became the centre of political activity, of classes every Sunday, of meetings of the different units. It became the place from where I worked for the next four years. I got to know the families living in the area. They were mainly of Punjabi origin and were living in this small colony of narrow lanes and poor civic facilities. I helped them petition the authorities on various issues with moderate success. We encouraged the residents to drop into the office if they required any help. I became almost like an adopted member of a Sikh family living there. The head of the family, Gyani Amar Singh, led a group of three who used to sing kirtans in the nearby gurudwaras. His wife, Bibi Gurbachan Kaur, cooked and cleaned, looking after her large brood. She had five daughters and three sons. The girls would come to our office to study, and I got to know the family well.

An important aspect of work as a secretary is the identification of potential cadre. Being involved in union work, I had a fairly good idea of the potential of many of the trade union workers. The economic burdens were such that it was difficult for them to give up their jobs and become wholetime Party workers. However, several of the politically more advanced workers did agree to take on responsibilities in building the Party in different workers' localities in north Delhi, even while they continued with their jobs. We spread to new areas because of their work. This method of building Party units in residential areas through contacts developed by mill workers was a good example of the classic form of communist organising, with workers as the fulcrum of the expansion of the Party and the development of socialist consciousness. We held classes on capitalism, the roots of the system of exploitation, and the cultures of the ruling classes, which marginalised the importance of workers' contributions. Several worker-activists developed, strengthening the base of the Party. We also developed new Party units in some industrial areas through struggles for minimum wages and against retrenchment. Our contacts in various colonies also did the same. We developed new cadre and brought them into the Party.

It was a good decision of the Delhi state committee to link

Party units among students at DU, adjacent to the Kamala Nagar office, to work with the local committee. In my experience, it is critical for the development of student cadre to introduce them to working-class areas and the issues and struggles connected with workers' lives. A lack of such direct experience can derail young cadre, as happened with many of the student leaders of the West in the aftermath of the heady days of the sixties. Subodh, for example, became a wholetime Party worker and was inducted into the local committee.

Fund Collection

There was a dearth of wholetime workers since it was difficult for workers to give up their jobs given their economic distress. It was mainly those who were dismissed because of union activity who could give more time, so ironically, we had to thank employers for all those who developed as wholetime cadre! As secretary, I felt that I should be doing much more to raise funds. We used to do what is referred to in Party parlance as 'box collection'. This consists of going shop-to-shop and house-to-house with tins and collecting money. We used to do this once a month.

The first time I did this kind of fund collection was in Calcutta with the student unit. We walked from the university to Chowringhee in the centre of the city with our tin boxes, collecting money. The following week, my elder sister Junie, with whom I was living at the time, got a call from my father. He had received a message from a horrified police commissioner, an old friend of my father's, who informed him that his daughter, in the company of 'certain dubious elements', was actually collecting funds from passers-by, and that too, holding a red flag! My exasperated father, who had not yet overcome his disapproval of my decision to join the Party, said to Junie, 'Really, does she have to do this, making a public spectacle of herself, in the heart of the city!' The fund collection drives in West Bengal were good training for my work in Delhi.

The other source of funds was a 'levy' paid by all Party members. The amount of levy a person paid was calculated in proportion to their income. Since our membership comprised low-paid industrial and textile workers, the levy was low and hardly enough to run an organisation. Prakash and I had the benefit of free accommodation given to us by the Party, but we just about managed to meet our modest expenses. I had no surplus money to help the Party with. I had lost all contacts with my old friends in Delhi who may have had the inclination and the capacity to help. When I look back, I think it was foolish of me to have done so, not so much because I could no longer ask them for donations to the Party but because I simply assumed that we had little in common. I realised how wrong I was decades later when I reconnected with some friends and learnt about the substantial work many of them had done for public good. I confess I had many such silly notions about how one 'declasses' oneself!

To take another example — I had pledged when I came back from London in 1970 that I would give up my passport and never go abroad till after the revolution. I guess I was not alone in believing in those days that the revolution was imminent. It was not until 2005, when I became a member of parliament and an automatic owner of a passport that I travelled abroad again. Meanwhile, the Soviet Union had collapsed, and I never got the opportunity to visit the first socialist country in the world — all due to my stubbornness! But I still strongly believe in the immediacy of the revolutionary goal. While it is true that the revolution is not around the corner, the immediacy of the goal means that every action, policy, plan, and struggle must be in the framework of that goal. Comrade BTR, in one of his profound observations, had said all tactics and no strategy will land you into collaboration with the Indian State, and all strategy and no tactics will end up with you on the mountain top with no contact with the people. How will what we do today link with our goal of achieving socialism? In my mind, in all these years of my work in the party and the movement, this has been a guiding principle.

Home Truths

The years of work as the secretary of the north Delhi committee laid the foundation for my future organisational work at various levels in the Party. It was not without its tensions, often arising out of inner-party discussions and differences. I also learnt the hard way how to take criticism. It's not easy to sit in a meeting and listen to harsh comments about one's work, one's style, and one's interactions. Comrades were often blunt and to the point, without niceties. You either learn to accept and deal with it or quit. This is the real declassing that takes place for a communist, a growing understanding that the individual and the ego can have little place if the mission is social change and revolution. The strength of the Party lies in developing the collective, and the person occupying the post of secretary of the unit, whether at the grassroots level or at the higher levels of responsibility of the party, has to set an example to subsume their individual likes and dislikes to the larger interest of the collective.

In my time as secretary, another home truth I learnt was the gap that existed between the struggles we led and the political dividend for us in terms of votes polled in elections. This is a larger question that the Left has to confront. I found that even in working-class areas, where our unions had strength and carried heft, where workers' families would come to us with their difficulties, we would poll lower numbers in municipal polls than even the memberships of our unions. In all those years, we could never translate our support into votes. The same workers who supported us at the gate and considered the red flag their friend and ally rarely voted for us; they thought we were 'good and honest' but not strong enough to win the seat. The truth is that despite all our efforts and the support we got, we could not build a political constituency among the workers.

To a large extent, we ourselves were responsible. At the time, we also had a mechanical understanding of class struggle. The social aspects of class struggle, the social composition of workers, the influence of regional groupings, of caste and patriarchy in prevailing ideologies, and the underlying communal currents were not addressed by us as part of an intrinsic part of class struggle. We somehow assumed that the unity engendered by struggle on common issues would automatically translate into class consciousness. Delhi, of course, is a melting pot of diverse cultures without any binding commonality, unlike linguistic states. A political intervention also requires the strong support of the middle classes, which in our case was restricted mainly to university campuses and a few middle-class unions. We weren't able to expand our reach beyond these.

In some ways, these problems continue to confront our movement, while the challenges before us have only grown with the rise of Hindutva and the neoliberal assault on the lives and livelihoods of working people. That, however, is a separate discussion.

The Last Shift Whistle

I conclude this section with a summary of what happened to the mills and the workers. The owners bled the mills dry, refused to reinvest their profits back into the mills, and used the profits for other ventures. They put more and more burdens of workload on the workers. They would fudge balance sheets to show losses and thereby escape paying statutory dues to the workers. In 1986, the workers were forced to go on another prolonged strike. They made some gains, notably a 53 rupees increase in the basic wage and an increase in DA, but the writing was on the wall. The owners wanted to close down the mills and use the land for real estate. The mills were located in the heart of the city, somewhat like the Mumbai mills, and what happened in Delhi broadly followed the Mumbai trajectory. The historic strike of the textile mill workers of Mumbai in 1982 under the leadership of Datta Samant had shaken the city, but the combined power and class alliance of the government, the owners, the police, and the collaborators' union, the Rashtriya Mill Mazdoor Sangh (RMMS), led to the defeat of the workers, despite all their courage and heroism. The mills got permission to use their costly land as real estate and started shutting down. Over the next decade, the city's landscape changed. The mills were history.

Taking their cue from Mumbai, mill owners in Delhi started giving notice to the government that they wanted to close the mills. The first to do so was DCM. In 1982, it filed applications stating that since the Delhi Master Plan 1962 had directed that all hazardous industries, such as the textile mills, had to be relocated or closed down, they wanted to close down unless they were given 150 acres where they could modernise and relocate. They asked for permission to 'develop' the 27 acres of the land where the mill was located. The mill's sister concerns, Swatantra Bharat Mills and DCM Silk were located on 38 acres of land. These, too, were to be closed and the land 'developed'. The Birla Mills had already started closing down various sections of the mill, including the weaving department, shifting its production gradually to power looms around Delhi.

Even as these cases were being contested in courts by the unions, a petition was filed by M.C. Mehta, an environmentalist lawyer who demanded that all industries defined in the Delhi Master Plan as polluting or hazardous should be closed. Nine thousand such units were identified, affecting over fifty thousand workers. This is an example of how interventions in the name of environment with no plan for alternative employment for those who will be affected lead to catastrophe in the lives of countless workers. By the end of the eighties, thousands of textile mills workers were retrenched. The departments started closing down one by one, the work being outsourced to spinning and power loom factories, which produced the cloth, which was then simply branded by the mills. The final Supreme Court orders for the closure of all the mills came in November 1996. By then, a majority of workers had already lost their employment. The Birla Mills shifted some of its operations to Baddi in Himachal Pradesh, but only a few score workers from Delhi joined this unit. Swatantra Bharat Mills opened some sections in Tonk in Rajasthan. It was claimed that the Supreme Court was 'fair' in that it increased the compensation from one year's wages to six years' wages. But what did it amount to? After decades of work, the majority of workers did not get even one lakh rupees. However, the land deals brought huge profits to the owners. The Swatantra Bharat Mills land was bought by DLF for Rs 1,582 crore in 2008. All mill owners raked in huge profits from the sale of land, which was their original intent anyway.

The relentless development of capitalism bulldozes the lives and livelihoods of millions of workers. Textile production could be achieved through outsourcing. It started with the power looms and small spinning units that employed workers at one-fourth the cost that the mills had paid. Today, it has all been replaced with highly automated looms. The development of productive forces should benefit workers, but under capitalism, it leads to unemployment and misery for workers. The land where the mills stood, the gates where thousands of workers passed through every day, have been replaced by high-rise apartments. The whistle for the shift to start stopped long ago.

Many of the workers left Delhi. We tried to keep in touch with them and involve them in the work of the Party in states where they had relocated. Some of the best, most political of the workers have passed away in these years. These include the main office bearers of the union — Changur, Inder Pal, Kamal Narayan, Roshan Lal, Ramesh, and Sarwan Kumar. They all continue to live on in our memories. I do sometimes meet those who are still in Delhi — Bishen Pal, Chhote Lal, Dayanand, Harish Chandra Pant, Nathu Parshad, Ram Pal, Sohan Lal, and Shiv Kumar — all of whom helped me to put together these memoirs. Dates may have blurred, but the vibrant experience of our struggles together is alive in each one of us. As are the lessons, at least for me, so many decades later.

IV

HERE COME THE WOMEN

Shifting Streams

A specific decision of the Jalandhar Party Congress (April 1978) was to have a direct impact on the course of my life, though I did not know it at the time. It concerned the discussions raised by women delegates on the importance of building a left-oriented national women's organisation. Only 24 of the 572 delegates and observers for the Congress were women, but those who spoke made their points effectively. I remember Ahilya Rangnekar and Vimal Ranadive, both freedom fighters, and Susheela Gopalan, all steeled in class struggle, passionately arguing in favour of building such an organisation, and asking the Party to back this organisation fully. This was subsequently confirmed by a special conference dedicated to organisational issues held in December 1978. By mid-1979, a coordination committee had been formed at the national level made up of women who were leading state-based women's organisations allied with the Left. This process culminated in the formation of the AIDWA in 1981.

The post-Emergency period in Delhi saw the birth and proliferation of women's groups who called themselves 'autonomous feminist groups'. They may have had differences among them, but what was common to them all was an undisguised contempt for the organised Left, whom they accused of 'subsuming gender to class'. I read some of their writing in newspapers and magazines, and our views did seem worlds apart. On the Left, we looked for the reasons behind women's unequal status in socio-economic frameworks, in government policies, and in the promotion of culture, which, in the name of tradition, glorified women's subjugation to men so that it was all the easier to exploit cheap female labour. Most of the autonomous groups, on the other hand, saw the world through a one-dimensional male vs female paradigm. Their theory of 'sisterhood' did not recognise the real objective differences amongst women due to their class and, in the Indian context, caste location. These groups seemed more interested in identifying all men as their enemies, and saw fighting capitalist exploitation as a diversion. It seemed to me that 'autonomy' for them meant autonomy from a deeper political and social analysis of women's status in a society such as ours.

I had no personal acquaintance with any of the groups. I knew that on the university campuses, particularly in JNU, there were heated discussions between women members of the SFI and activists of the 'autonomous' women's movements. I had met some of the SFI women students as part of the big group from JNU who had come to the DCM gate during the bonus strike in 1978. But there was little contact after that, and I was not part of any of those debates.

I was, therefore, surprised when one day in April or May 1979, Major summoned me for what he said was an important meeting. When I got to the office, I found two young women there with him, Indu Agnihotri and Meera Velayadhun, both from JNU. Indu, the more assertive of the two, slight with long hair and glasses, spoke passionately, while Meera, equally articulate, spoke in measured words about the importance of the Left. They spoke eloquently of the need for a stronger Left intervention in the developing women's movement in the capital of building such a women's organisation. Neither of them was a member of the Party, but their experience of working with other women's groups had convinced them of the need for a more class-based approach. Major expressed his unequivocal agreement and explained to them how the Party, too, had decided to support such efforts. He looked at me, expecting a response. What Indu and Meera said resonated with me, but I was a reluctant participant in the discussion because I guessed that Major was keen that I get involved. My own inclination was to remain where I was, in the local committee work and trade union work in north Delhi.

In June of that year, Major took the discussion further through a decision in the Party state committee that I would be given the responsibility to work out a plan for building a women's organisation in Delhi. This would become Janwadi Mahila Samiti (JMS), the Delhi unit of what was to become the AIDWA. I said that I was involved in preparing for the textile workers' strike and it would be difficult for me to do this, but the decision remained unchanged. I could not really follow up on it till after the strike was resolved in September 1979.

I think time was kind to me. It stretched to allow me to embark on this journey of learning and discovery, a new path for me, while continuing to shoulder my responsibilities in the union and the party. My work with women had been so far linked to my union work and the political work of the Party. In my life till then, it was the workers who were the protagonists. My frequent discussions with Indu and Meera and an expanded group of women from JNU and DU over the next few months led to a slow shifting of my perspectives toward understanding the multiple dimensions of women's exploitation and oppression in a capitalist society.

Organising the Organisers

We formed an organisation committee to take the work forward. There were nine of us: Ashalata, Chachi (Chacha's wife), Indu, Meera, Nishat Siddique (who taught in a government school in Delhi), Omvati (Amma) from the Birla Mills community, Ranjana, Shanti from Azadpur, and I as the convenor. I was involved in renewing the contacts we had made over the years in workers' and resettlement colonies. The union network was a critical factor, with workers taking the initiative of giving us new contacts in the areas where they lived. Women students from JNU also came from time to time. They were active on campus, holding seminars, exhibitions, and protests.

It was because of their initiatives and struggles that a large group of us from north Delhi participated in the historic united march on International Women's Day 1980 against the Supreme Court judgement in the appalling Mathura rape case. Mathura, a minor Adivasi girl, was raped in custody at a police station in 1972. The trial court exonerated the policemen with the statement that this Adivasi teenager, barely fourteen years old, was 'habituated to sexual intercourse'. The Bombay High Court reversed this judgement and sentenced the policemen to five years' imprisonment. However, in September 1979, the Supreme Court reversed the sentence, arguing that since Mathura had not raised an alarm, since there were no physical marks of her fight against being raped, it could be concluded that she had consented to sexual intercourse. We were shocked and outraged. Women's organisations and groups strongly protested. Four eminent lawyers petitioned the Supreme Court against the judgement. In the capital, the historic march was led by Lotika Sarkar, Upendra Baxi,

(Left to right) Ranjana, Ashoka, Chachi, Chachi's granddaughter, Rita, Sulochana.

and others who were petitioners in the case. We also requested workers and trade unions to join. Hundreds of workers mobilised by CITU joined the march. It was a logical extension of our efforts to gather wider support for our fight against sexual violence. That movement grew into a massive nationwide sustained struggle to reform the wholly biased laws against rape.

We built area-wise networks, giving responsibilities to our earlier contacts to organise local meetings. Gita(Dayanand's wife), Omvati/Amma, Prasanni of the handloom workers, Shanti, and Vijay, a Bengali woman we had met in Nand Nagri along with Razia — all working-class women, organised meetings in the areas where they lived. It was exciting to see how many of the women whom I had met in the early days of my work in north Delhi developed into organisers. Prasanni, who spun cotton on a charkha, was unlettered. She belonged to a poor, scheduled caste family and had hardly any contact with the world outside her family and her colony of Sawan Park. She started attending our group meetings and decided that more women should participate because she felt we were discussing issues relevant to their lives. Before every meeting, she would go around the colony mobilising women. When women asked her why they should join, she started giving brief extempore speeches. She told me she enjoyed doing so and added with a mischievous smile, 'I think I am as good as Pradhanji in giving speeches'. 'Pradhanji' was her husband, Sarwan Kumar, president of the handloom workers union! She was soon elected as the president of the JMS unit in Sawan Park and became one of the most active members of the organisation.

Another example was that of Omvati/Amma. She had led the struggle against strike- breakers at the Birla Mills. She was a widow who had taken up outsourced work of various kinds to bring up her two sons. To her distress, however, the joint family broke up. She shifted with her elder son, Suresh, to their new home in the Mangolpuri resettlement colony. It was in 1980 that I visited her. I found her depressed and lonely. She missed her old life in the Birla Mills workers' colony. I suggested that she join our effort to build a women's organisation. She didn't agree at first because, according to her, she had no patience! She did eventually join and used to regularly hold meetings at her home, although she was a better fighter on the street than in a women's meeting.

We held numerous meetings across Delhi in the next six months. The number of women activists slowly increased. Our efforts were to develop women activists from the unit level. We organised regular classes on a wide range of issues, such as — the roots of women's oppression and patriarchy, the reasons for economic inequality, why some people are rich and others poor, the use of tradition and customs to reinforce women's subordinate status, the meaning of women's emancipation. Babli Gupta, Indu, Meera, and many others used to go regularly to different corners of Delhi where our units were being formed to take classes for women, most of whom had never had the opportunity to go to school.

When I look back at those days, I believe the effort made to develop activists at the local level was a critical step in building the organisation. Unlike many of the funded NGOs, we had no resources to help women financially, so women came voluntarily to our meetings. It was extraordinary how the women, facing multifarious challenges at home and outside, developed into activists, into comrades, motivated by their commitment to social change. Cultural restrictions prevented women from expressing their personalities in the public space. Many of them used to cover their heads with the end of their sarees and were hesitant to speak in front of the senior male members of their families. Culture is often the most stubborn barrier to breach.

It is obvious that for women's leadership to develop, women had to be recognised as leaders by men, too. They faced many problems. A common complaint was gossip about them in the neighbourhood. They would hear snide comments like, 'So and so's wife is always seen in the company of other men; she is out of control', or 'Where is she going every day, without an escort'. It was not unusual for their husbands to react and prevent them from leaving the house. In such cases, sometimes one of us would go and meet the husband or mother-in-law and talk to them about our organisation. But mostly, the women fought it out by themselves.

A young woman who joined the student movement at DU, Kamla, had a self-choice marriage with a fellow activist, Yashpal. Their marriage was opposed by their families, even though both belonged to Scheduled Caste communities, though following different sects. Kamla and Yashpal somehow overcame the families' opposition. After their marriage, Kamla moved into her husband's joint family home in a colony adjoining Sawan Park. She soon joined the women's organisation and emerged as a key leader of the movement. She was often out of her home all day, involved in organisational work. A few months after her marriage, her father-in-law told her that he was fed up with hearing comments from 'the community' about her 'attending meetings with men unknown to the family' and forbade her from doing activist work. Kamla rebelled. Her father-in-law summoned her father and complained to him. Yashpal was warned, too, but Kamla stood firm and refused to quit her organising work. There was an uneasy truce, but eventually, her work was recognised by the in-laws. In fact, a few years later, she and I were among the fourteen women who were arrested and sent to jail for protesting the hike in the price of milk. Many of them, like Kamla, were activists who had confronted and overcome familial opposition to their work. By then, Kamla had become a mother with a one-year-old daughter. I said that maybe she should stay on the sidelines of the demonstration in case the police baton-charged us. But she said that Yashpal would be there to look after the child, and anyway, it was good training for him! We stayed together in a large cell. We organised games for the inmates, cooked, and ate together. We were given bail after four days. I had been to jail earlier, but for the rest, it was their first time. They were quite nonchalant about it, though!

Setting Up Units

Women's movements have played a big part in building an environment for women's participation in public life. The reservation of seats for women in local bodies was a result of women's struggles for political representation. There is now a wider social sanction for women to express themselves, to speak in neighbourhood meetings in front of audiences of men and women. But it was not so at the time. Many of our activists broke these barriers, and with the help and support of the organisation, they began expressing their opinions publicly. So, in a way, these working-class women who joined Left women's movements were pioneers in bringing the poorer sections of women into agitational politics and in the process, they also developed as leaders.

I felt a deep respect and love for them and realised how much I was enjoying my work. We also had so much fun together. It was a different world for them, away from the male gaze. We sometimes had singing and dancing sessions. There were many women who played the drum, the desi dholak, really well. With the rhythmic beat of the drum, they would twirl around and dance with abandon. At social functions, particularly at a wedding, the singing in the women's sections was quite risqué, as were the dance gestures; they would give Bollywood stars a run for their money! The children squatting on the ground would form a circle, watching wide-eyed, perhaps wondering at the transformation of their mothers, usually so silent and demure. I enjoyed these outings and would often be pulled into the circle of the dancing women.

In our meetings, working-class women raised the concerns of poor, urban women. Scarce water supply was a common issue, with women having to spend hours in queues at the too few water

Indu Agnihotri (with microphone), Rajni Palriwala (behind Indu, left), Meera Velayudhan (behind Indu, right) and others campaigning for transport facilities for women, Nand Nagri.

hand pumps. Public transport was another issue. Women factory workers would complain that buses were so crowded that they had to leave home much earlier in order to get to work on time, making their day a twelve-hour day. Getting ration cards to avail of the public distribution system was also a big issue.

We organised demonstrations in the localities and before local and district authorities. Alongside this, we started a membership campaign. Groups of us would go house to house, talking to residents and explaining our aims of equality and justice. By July 1980, we had 1,000 members and were ready to form elected unit committees in different areas. The process comprised holding meetings of our members locality-wise and asking them to elect a secretary, a president, and a committee. We could achieve this in around nine to ten areas. The first state-level demonstration we held under the JMS banner was in October 1980 when over five hundred women, mainly from the working classes, marched to Boat Club with our charter of demands. It was a proud moment for all of us.

New Comrades

It was around this time that our team was strengthened with the addition of another student from JNU, Ashoklata Jain ('Ashoka'). I have spoken earlier of her role in the resistance to the Emergency in JNU. She was suspended and later expelled from the university but continued to lead the SFI. In JNU, she had met Prabir Purkayastha, also an SFI leader, and the two got romantically involved. They decided to get married and, in fact, gave notice of their marriage to the marriage registrar, as they were legally required to do. Their love story was alas rudely interrupted by Prabir's arrest soon after the Emergency was declared. His arrest became an example of the arbitrary and opaque nature of the process of detention. For six days, the intelligence wing of Delhi Police could not provide the grounds for his detention. As the police later admitted, they had zero evidence against him. He spent nearly the entirety of the Emergency in jail, first in Tihar and then in Agra. They got married only after he was released.

After their marriage, Prabir and Ashoka decided that one of them would become a Party wholetimer, and the other would earn for the couple. They discussed this with the Party. It was somehow assumed in such situations that the husband would become the wholetimer and the wife would earn. But Prakash, who was in charge of the JNU unit of the Party, and Major, the state secretary, between them decided that it was time this patriarchal norm was challenged. Prabir fully supported Ashoka's decision and saw no reason to challenge the party's opinion. Thus, Ashoka became a wholetimer of the Party and an incredibly valuable member of our team. She took on the responsibility of working in west Delhi and plunged with gusto into working with the textile workers

Ashoka, leading an AIDWA demonstration. Ranjana is in the foreground. This photo was shot by Safdar Hashmi.

from SBM and DCM Silk and in and around the Mangolpuri resettlement colony. She played a leading role in establishing new Party units in these areas.

Towards the end of 1980, we established a legal aid cell. This gave a boost to the organisation's work. It was set up at the initiative of Kirti Singh, a former DU students' activist-turned-lawyer. She was committed to Left politics, and when she learnt of the formation of JMS, she contacted us and gave her time and advice with unstinted generosity and dedication. She made a big difference to the work. At the time, we did not have an office and were working out of the narrow veranda attached to the state centre of the CITU office. Kirti started a *pro bono* counselling centre every Saturday, which dealt mainly with cases of domestic violence. Through this centre, many of our area-level activists were trained as effective counsellors. Every week, we would get cases referred to us from different areas. An early decision we took was that we should get neighbourhood support for the victim in the case. This was not easy because neighbours would be afraid to antagonise

147

Brinda with Kalindi in the late 1990s. Behind them is Chenni.

the husband or the in-laws of the girl. However, we encouraged the woman complainant to build social support among her own contacts and to introduce them to the organisation.

Many of the women who came to JMS with personal cases developed into activists. I would adjust my schedule and make it a point to be present at the Saturday sessions to ensure organisational follow-up and support to the legal assistance in individual cases. Slowly, the Saturday counselling sessions developed into an important centre, which drew many more activists from the areas who took on responsibilities. Kirti also initiated discussions within the organisation in Delhi on the infirmities of the laws dealing with cases of dowry and rape. We were her eager students, learning how to read between the lines of legalese, which often concealed patriarchal bias. She drafted suggestions for amendments to the anti-dowry and anti-rape laws, which were supported by many other organisations and which formed the basis for our representations before the parliamentary committees formed for this purpose in 1980.

The following year, in 1981, we held a meeting of professors and students whom we had been in contact with. There were about 20-odd people in this meeting, and most of them went on to become active in JMS in some capacity or other subsequently. A highlight of that meeting was a presentation on the different aspects of dowry by Utsa Patnaik, professor of economics at JNU. I remember the meeting for another reason as well. Accompanying Utsa was Kalindi Deshpande, who went on to become an extremely committed and effective leader of the organisation in Delhi, as well as my close personal friend.

Kalindi's story is instructive in that it shows how we are sometimes insensitive to recognising people's talent and potential. She was married to prominent Marxist intellectual and celebrated Marathi playwright G.P. Deshpande. The couple lived on the JNU campus with their two children. Their house was a sort of adda where intellectuals and artists would often meet and discuss politics and art. Kalindi was a superb cook, and while guests complimented her on the food, nobody thought of including her in the discussions. She felt sort of excluded from the circle. Utsa realised that Kalindi had a keen interest in social and political issues and asked if she'd like to come along for the JMS meeting. Kalindi would later laugh and tell me how, as she became more and more active politically, it was her views that were the most sought by the intellectuals since she was the only one who worked at the ground level.

Breaking Barriers

It was the coming together of two streams — the Left student movement, represented by committed women activists, and working-class women influenced by class struggles — that resulted in the birth and growth of the JMS in Delhi. The impact on me, as a part of this process, was profound. Working with women transformed me in so many ways. I realised that to understand the brutality of class exploitation, you need to understand both the lives of working women and the lives of wives of workers. The lives of wives of workers are sadly not studied enough by those who seek to analyse capitalism, even though their struggle and strategies for survival in the reproductive economy make them anything but passive onlookers.

The intensive work I did along with others in the first year opened my eyes to a 'poor woman's world'. Just as I had educated myself about textile workers' issues and cultures by spending hours at mill gates, here I was in the homes of working people, talking exclusively to women. But it was difficult too. I found that many of them had deeply conservative views. Their attitudes towards their daughters or their daughters-in-law, were often coloured by patriarchal notions, reflected, for example, in son-preference practices. Demands for dowry were spreading rapidly among working-class families, even in those communities where the practice of dowry had been traditionally muted. We raised these issues in meetings and encouraged discussions around them. We found that holding these small group meetings of, say, ten or fifteen women, though a time-consuming process, helped women understand our organisation and its approach better and helped them to relate to the organisation as their own.

We also came across cases of domestic violence and wife beating. It was the first time I was coming face-to-face with the suffering and humiliation that a woman victim of domestic violence faces, and the fear, the loss of self-confidence, the insecurity she confronts. In poor families, it was even more difficult for a woman to leave her marital home because she felt guilty about the economic burden that would entail for her parents. It was not so much the social stigma but the economic aspect that concerned her. I felt rage against the cruelties of such practices born of male privilege embedded in our social relations. It is true that domestic violence cuts across religion, caste, and class, but I think it affected me particularly when I encountered it in working-class families. I felt the Party and our trade unions needed to be more conscious of and sensitised to these realities. I would wonder: how can we speak of working-class culture as an alternative unless we include the issues of equal and democratic inter-family relations between men and women in working-class families?

Having said that, my experience is that in comparison to middle-class families, the men in working-class families were more open to discussion, counselling, and change around issues of domestic violence, even in families that experienced it. I remember a worker from ATM. For a week after he got his wages, he would go on a drinking binge and, upon returning home, would abuse and beat up his wife and terrorise the children. This issue came up in a neighbourhood meeting organised in the Azadpur area by Shanti and Maya, a new member of the organisation. The women decided they would confront him and warn him that the next time he misbehaved with his wife, they would beat him up. When he inevitably got drunk the next time, he was confronted by a group of angry women led by Maya, who literally threw him out of his own house. Some of the women stayed with his wife for the next couple of days. This became the talk of the mill. Our male comrades, who were sceptical about such actions earlier, were now happy to support the women and claim credit! They negotiated

Left to right: Shanti, Rita, a comrade, Chachi and Vimal Ranadive at a protest action in 1981 in connection with the Rameeza Bee case. Rameeza Bee was raped by four policemen in 1978 and her husband, Ahmad Hussain, was beaten up for protesting, leading to his death. The police claimed that Rameeza Bee was a 'prostitue' and Ahmad Hussain her pimp. His death triggered widespread protests and violence in Hyderabad. The case highlighted the misogyny and prurience of the media, the legal system, and public discourse, as well as the suffering, the lived realities, and the denial of justice that poor Muslims faced routinely.

with the management and ensured that the wife, with the reluctant agreement of her husband who was sober at the time, got the main part of the wage. This ultimately changed her husband's behaviour. Later, when our work expanded to middle-class areas, I found a marked difference. Women were far less able to raise issues of domestic violence, burdened by social stereotyping of how 'good women' should be, 'adjustment' to violence being the expected norm. In workers' families, women spoke out more. Also, there were far fewer cases — hardly any, actually — that we came across of dowry murders in working-class families.

Initially, when I raised these issues in meetings of the Party local committee, and sometimes in the union, the reactions were mixed. While some were supportive, others felt that by raising 'family' matters, we would be dividing the working class, thereby weakening the struggle. They preferred that we focussed on issues that women raised against government policy. On the other hand, when we organised workers in a struggle against employers, we received the full support of the Party and the union. For some comrades, questioning relations within the 'core' of social structures, the 'sacrosanct family' was taboo. It took many discussions and women's assertion to change attitudes.

Crimes against women are often made invisible. Sometimes, dramatic and militant actions are necessary to break the silence. We organised several such actions. One was in Karnataka Bhavan in New Delhi in July 1981. The Karnataka home minister's brother was accused of rape, but the government, far from initiating investigation and action against him, was defending him. We heard that the home minister had come to Delhi and was staying at Karnataka Bhavan. Seventy or eighty of us barged into the building, where a sympathetic staff member gave us directions to his room. We did a 'gherao' for several hours, not allowing the minister to leave his room, and succeeded in bringing public attention to the case.

There is little doubt in my mind that the formation of a women's organisation had a significant impact within the Party. To be sure, the process started slowly. There were two factors. The first was women's assertion within the Party. The second was the undeniable force for change represented by the issues being raised by the united women's movement. Till then, issues connected with women's unequal status were generalised to the extent that there was no immediacy attached to working for change. After the Working Women's Coordination Committee was formed in 1979, a churning process began in the trade unions. Simultaneously, the development of the united women's movement in the eighties had an impact within the Party, too. Today, nobody can seriously argue that the issue of, say, domestic violence is not to be taken seriously. But at the time, we were breaking barriers — just as those who came before us did in their context, and younger comrades today are doing in their context.

The Anti-Dowry Campaign

One day in October 1980, I was at the Party office in Roshanara Bagh when our neighbour, Gyani Amar Singh, came in, highly distressed. His eldest daughter, Surinder Kaur (fondly called Chenni), had somehow smuggled out an urgent message that her husband had beaten her up, then locked her and refused to give her food. I knew Chenni was a few months pregnant. I had met her when she had visited her parents a month earlier. She had complained of domestic violence even then. I had asked her to leave her husband's home. Her parents were also supportive. But like many women in such distressing situations, she felt she would be a burden on her parents, and continued to bear with the violence.

Ashalata and I rushed to the JJ Colony in Wazirpur, where Chenni lived. We had contacts in the colony and were able to quickly mobilise about thirty women. Her husband was not at home, but her fierce mother-in-law was. She was livid and refused to let us meet Chenni. Some women who lived in that lane came out in support of their neighbour. It was quite a scene — women versus women. We stood our ground and refused to leave without Chenni. The police arrived but refused to lodge our complaint — a typical stance. An hour or so went by while the confrontation continued. Now, some women in the lane had started supporting us. Eventually, the mother-in-law allowed three of us to enter the house. I was heartbroken and infuriated to see Chenni crouched on the floor, badly bruised, weeping. We took her home. She recovered with the loving care of her parents and siblings and became a regular at the Roshanara Bagh office. She delivered a beautiful girl child unharmed by the beatings Chenni had faced.

She was named Kranti, Revolution. Chenni developed into a front-ranking activist, helping expand the organisation into new areas and assisting other women in distress.

I was listed as a witness in Chenni's case. We were in court one day, and the hearing had just started. As soon as I walked in, her husband's lawyer said loudly to the magistrate, 'Here she is, the woman who breaks families'. I was shocked and about to retort when our lawyer warned me, 'You have to follow the protocol, or you will be charged with contempt of court'. The magistrate did not reprimand the misogynist lawyer. We faced this kind of hostility in the courts quite often.

We formed a roving squad that would follow up on cases that were reported in the newspapers. The members of this squad were students, teachers, and other professionals based in south Delhi. Kalindi was the convenor of the squad. Among the members was a young woman, Manjari, training to be a lawyer. She would check all the press reports and ensure that the cases were followed up. I remember one case that showed us what was possible. A young woman, Rita Chaddha, was set afire by her husband's family and suffered 70 per cent burns. Miraculously, she survived. Her family contacted us. They said that Rita was no longer going to live with her in-laws, but they were refusing to return the dowry. We organised a demonstration to the in-laws' home in Kirti Nagar in west Delhi in January 1982. Within an hour, they agreed to return the dowry worth over one lakh rupees, a large sum in those days. This was the first such case in the capital where the entire dowry was returned to the girl's family.

A recurring pattern in domestic and dowry violence was the protection given by the police to the accused — hardly surprising, given how much patriarchal thinking pervaded police culture. In 1980, there were 255 reported cases of dowry murders in Delhi. In virtually every case, the police put out the 'stove burst' theory — that the young bride was cooking, the kerosene stove burst and her clothes caught fire. It is true that the kerosene stoves of those days were badly designed and often prone to malfunction or accidents. But to believe that stoves had a propensity to burst only when young brides used them invariably would have been laughable, but it was an argument that was used by the police for their misogynist inaction. This fiction was manufactured by the in-laws in cahoots with the police. As a result, many of our protests were directed against the police.

We also had many run-ins with the courts, which were also often quite regressive in their approach — with some sterling exceptions. An example that demonstrated both sides of the judiciary was the infamous Sudha Goel case of 1983. The young bride had been burnt and murdered. The trial court had pronounced the guilty verdict against the accused. The Delhi High Court not only overturned that verdict but also held that receiving and giving dowry was a 'customary Hindu practice'. We were infuriated. Along with other women's organisations, we protested against the judgement. We scaled the walls of the court complex and jumped in. We created a lot of noise and ruckus. Some lawyers filed a contempt of court case against us. We decided that we would defend ourselves and use the court as a platform for our arguments. Suman Krishna Kant, leader of the Mahila Dakshata Samiti, and I, on behalf of the JMS, argued before the court. I did enjoy that experience! It was to our advantage that we had a bench comprising Justices Leila Seth and Rajinder Sachar, both known, through various judgements, for their sensitivity to social and democratic issues. They gave us the opportunity to put across our arguments as to why the Court judgement had to be criticised. We got substantial coverage in the press. At every hearing, JMS activists would fill the courtroom. Our opposing lawyers would protest this, but the court did not object. Tutored by Kirti, I had to study the contours of legal arguments and precedents before every hearing. We agreed that my interventions had to raise broader social and political issues linked to our movement against dowry. In the end, we were declared guilty of contempt of court. Our punishment? We were asked to remain in court till the court rose! It was a small price to pay for getting the opportunity to turn a case against us into a platform to highlight the issues of the movement.

In another case, we had been contacted by a domestic worker whose nine-year-old child had been raped by her employer's son. They were Dalits, and the worker had often faced casteist abuse. The police registered a rape case, but refused to register a case under the SC/ST Act. We demonstrated, we petitioned, and under Kirti's initiative, we fought it out in court, but although the man was convicted of rape, the caste abuse was ignored. The caste dimension in several cases of sexual assault against Dalit women was deliberately concealed by the police, and the courts rarely intervened. We encountered this repeatedly.

The JMS Way

When JMS was formally set up in Delhi at its first conference in 1981, Ashoka became its founder president and I, the general secretary. Our committee expanded to 25 members representing different areas of the city. JMS rapidly developed a profile as a militant women's organisation, committed to fighting for women's rights, and soon became Delhi's largest women's organisation. Behind this success was the collective leadership that developed at different levels, and especially at the state centre. We knew each other's strengths and limitations, and worked together as a team.

I believe that there were five pillars to the culture that developed at different levels of our work in JMS. First, we sought to understand the issue being addressed in all its dimensions. This meant research both at the ground level and by reading the literature around it. We also often consulted experts who had worked in the area. Second, we recognised the necessity of quick and timely intervention in various cases. If a woman was being harassed for dowry or was murdered, one had to move swiftly before the perpetrators, often with the help of the police, could cover up their actions or tamper with evidence. Our swift action could also be the difference between life and death for the victim. But not just in cases of sexual violence. In other issues also, interventions have to be timely. It is only then that the action can have an impact. Third, we had to develop the ability and capacity to take risks in militant protests, when the situation demanded it. In most cases, this meant confrontation with the police. There are numerous occasions when JMS activists have had to face lathi charges and get water cannoned when our protests were disallowed.

In one of the demonstrations in support of a Bharat Bandh call in the late eighties, my right arm was smashed and broken by a policeman at the Connaught Place police station. The broken bones did not set properly, and I have the mark of it even today. I remember a photograph which depicted the bravery of one of our activists, Molina, a domestic worker in south Delhi. It was a protest against price rise, and we were breaking through the police barrier. The water cannon was aimed directly at her, and she was literally lifted off the ground, and since she was holding on to the barricade, she was parallel to the ground. She was badly hurt but came back to the next protest as soon as she was better. So personal courage was also an important element in our building the organization. Fourth, we had to learn to take up organisational work and responsibilities proactively. We developed a culture where the words 'No, I can't take this responsibility' were absolutely taboo. Everyone pitched in for all the work; no organisation can grow if everyone keeps waiting for someone else to take the lead. Above all, we believed it is commitment to an ideology which can inspire people to work, and it was left-wing thinking with a class-based analysis which informed our everyday work and which we tried to impart to our activists at every level.

The JMS was and is an organisation which has a multi-class base, multi-community base. Even in the early days, we strove to take up issues of all sections of women — common issues that a woman faces. But our work taught us that sisterhood is not a concept which should be interpreted as a biological basis for unity among women. This is a convenient veil to conceal deep class, and in the context of India, deep caste, not just differences but animosity and often hostility between women themselves. Our experience taught us that sisterhood would have meaning only if middle-class women would come out in solidarity with poor women or dominant caste women would break casteist cultures and support the struggle against caste oppression and violence because a woman was a Dalit. I strongly felt that in whatever capacity we worked and in whichever mass organisation, whether amongst students, youth, or other sections, the focus always had to be on the poor, the workers, their families, and on basti dwellers, among Dalit women. This doesn't mean one neglects the middle classes. On the contrary, it means working among the middle classes with the perspective of bringing them closer to the struggles of the working poor. This is hard, often unrewarding, invisible work. But if we, as communists, do not foreground the reality of class and caste inequality between women themselves and work towards unity based on the needs of the most oppressed and exploited sections of women, who will?

Through these early endeavours to build the organisational backbone of JMS, Major Saheb — as the secretary of the Delhi State Committee of the CPI(M) — was our anchor. He was always encouraging and always supportive in the discussions in the Party. Alas, in January 1982, while attending the Vijayawada Party Congress, he died following a massive cardiac arrest. The Party suffered a tragic and grievous loss with the death of our beloved state secretary. He was an extraordinary leader, uncompromising in his commitment to Marxism and communist organisational principles, yet with a sensitivity towards human frailty, which made him one of the least judgemental leaders I have known. The Party lost a leader who had so much still to contribute, particularly in the Hindi-speaking regions. For his legions of admirers, including me, his death was a huge personal loss. He was cremated in Vijayawada.

I will never forget the moment when we went to receive his life partner and Comrade Usha at Delhi airport. She had been a cultural artist in Assam and had met Major in his underground days before Independence. She came towards us, her face streaked with tears, her arms outstretched to the waiting, sombre, grieving crowd. The sound of suppressed sobbing suddenly transformed into a powerful slogan even though in broken voices: 'Red salute, Comrade Major!', *'Comrade Major amar rahein'* (Long live Comrade Major).

Comrade Major Jaipal Singh, a hero and legend in his lifetime, has remained for me an inspiration decades after his death.

Joint Movements and Struggles

In the following phase of our work, we participated in many joint movements with other women's organisations. The AIDWA, of which JMS was the Delhi unit, was formed in 1981 following the Mathura case. This was the time we were also involved in the anti-dowry struggle. Ashoka and I were elected to the central executive committee of AIDWA. Susheela Gopalan, a CPI(M) member of parliament from Kerala, was elected national general secretary, and the all-India centre was managed by her along with Vimal Ranadive, who was elected vice president.

At that time, three women MPs — Geeta Mukherjee (CPI), Pramila Dandavate (Janata Party), and Susheela Gopalan (CPI(M)) — formed a kind of trio in the Lok Sabha, raising the voices of women fighting in the streets against violence, dowry, and rape. Five women's organisations — AIDWA, National Federation of Indian Women (NFIW), Mahila Dakshata Samiti, Young Women's Christian Association (YWCA), and Centre for Women's Development Studies (CWDS) — came together to form a joint platform to demand changes in the laws related to rape and dowry. Later, this expanded into the Dahej Virodhi Chetna Manch (DVCM) with over fifty organisations and groups representing a wide range of social and professional sections. Since much of the planning and mobilisation for the joint actions had to be done in Delhi, the local units of these organisations were also included in the organisation committee. Thus, we from JMS began representing AIDWA in these meetings.

It was such a contrast from the joint trade union meetings I had attended for the textile workers' struggles. There, the politics was clear. Even the collaborationist trade unions found it difficult to avoid criticism of the government of the day. Nobody questioned the fact that struggles had to be conducted against the pro-employer government policies. In the meetings of the women's organisations, it was entirely different. The prevalent trend was to keep the movement 'above and away' from politics. Thus, any criticism of, say, the refusal of the government — at the time headed by Indira Gandhi — to make changes in the laws was considered 'political'. Even the phrase 'capitalist cultures' that promote dowry was seen as taboo. We countered this argument by saying that we would not use the word 'patriarchy' unless it was linked to socio-economic systems such as capitalism! We took turns attending the joint meetings — Ashoka, Indu Agnihotri, Kirti Singh, Meera Velayudhan, and myself, and sometimes Rajni Palriwala and Sahba Hussain, both active members of the JMS and well-versed in the interventions that were required. Once, Kirti, who had attended one of these meetings, came back totally fed up and said, 'I can't bear it; we have to fight for each word!'. Through all this was the calmness of Vina Mazumdar, a pioneer in women's studies who, along with Lotika Sarkar, had founded CWDS. In the years after 1975, when she had so generously opened her home for our wedding, I had not met her. This time, I saw her as a leading figure in the battle for gender equality and equity. She seemed to enjoy the heated debates, puffing away on her cigarette, and would then come up with a solution acceptable to everyone. She was a source of strength and knowledge and played a vital part in building the joint movement in Delhi, which had a wider influence throughout the country.

Throughout 1982 and part of 1983, the DVCM played an extremely important role in framing the issues around dowry through joint struggles, which included scores of street corner meetings. DVCM distributed lakhs of leaflets in all parts of Delhi and held meetings, seminars, and demonstrations. The JMS team was a crucial part of this campaign, perhaps the one organisation which sent teams to every corner of the city. On 3 August 1982, there was a huge march in Delhi, which was joined by thousands of citizens from all walks of life. Men, women, and children marched for social reform centred on women's rights. Ranjana Kumari from Mahila Dakshata Samiti, Primila Loomba from NFIW, and I from AIDWA were given responsibility for handling the stage. By then, we had a good rapport between us, and it all went smoothly. We were elated at the large gathering to support the demands of the women's movement.

The united movement succeeded in pushing for the formation of parliamentary committees to make changes in the laws related to rape and dowry, adopted by parliament in 1983. DVCM gave birth to another joint platform of national women's organisations. It consisted of AIDWA, AIWC, CWDS, Joint Women's Programme, Mahila Dakshata Samiti, NFIW, and YWCA — Vina Mazumdar had christened them the 'seven sisters'. This joint platform worked together during the decades of the eighties and nineties and not only made critical interventions on government policies but tread a path which, to a substantial extent, saved India's women's movements from the ideological trap of a 'women's only signboard' which proved fatal for the mainstream women's organisations in the West. We took up issues of joint concern with democratic and secular-minded citizens, men and women. For example, in the late eighties and nineties, on the issue of sectarian religious-based mobilisations by majoritarian forces in the agitations which led to the demolition of the Babri Masjid, the joint platform of the seven sisters had a robust response. We organised numerous campaigns against communalism. Earlier, in the immediate post-Emergency period, it would have been difficult to convince others of the importance of taking up broader issues, but experience taught us all the necessity of such interventions.

The Political is Personal

The sustained joint agitations we organised under the banner of the DVCM taught us how to unite despite differences. We also learnt to respect each other. At a personal level, I developed many friendships with those I had worked with in the joint movements, especially Primila Loomba and Mary Khemchand, then secretary of YWCA. In the broader group, too, we learnt enough about each other's positions to be able to negotiate and reach common ground without rancour. The learnings went beyond the individuals involved. I feel that the movement as a whole matured because of joint struggles. I can say with certainty that close contacts with the autonomous feminist groups helped us in the left-oriented women's movement to give more importance to inequalities within the family. And I hope that the autonomous feminist groups would agree that they became more political as a result of their interactions with us on the Left. 'The personal is political' was a popular slogan of the time, particularly with the autonomous feminist groups. Vina Mazumdar would urge, 'If the personal is political, make the political personal'.

1975–1985 was declared by the United Nations as the decade for women. It was observed both jointly and independently by women's organisations in Delhi. It gave us the opportunity within the joint movement to raise issues of the impact of economic policies on women — the situation of working women, women's employment and work conditions, budget allocations for matters of direct interest to women such as water supplies, housing, girls' education, and so on. The issues we were raising were political in the sense of situating women in the socio-economic political context of the society in which they lived and gave a new dimension to the united movement.

An important contribution of the joint movement of women's organisations and the broader platforms created was the impact on mainstream politics and political parties. The debates in parliament, the actions on the streets, the militant demonstrations and clashes with the police were widely reported in the media, which helped publicise the issues. In that post-Emergency period, many young women had joined the media who were regularly reporting on the protests. There is little doubt that the media played an important role — quite a contrast with the lack of media space for serious social issues today.

Political parties could no longer ignore or shelve women's issues as 'soft'. Many political parties developed their women's wings. This helped to raise issues of women within political parties. Certainly, in the Delhi CPI(M), the need for the party to walk the talk as far as raising and supporting the issues highlighted by the women's movement was recognised, and this, in turn, helped women within the Party. Many women joined the Party. This process continues till today.

A Grievous Loss

On 3 October 1983, a terrible tragedy struck. An entire world of shared experiences, struggles, friendship, learning, joy, and laughter lay shattered. Our beloved Ashoka died of a spontaneous brain haemorrhage. The end came suddenly, without any warning, in the middle of the night. She was thirty-three and healthy. She had recently, in August, given birth to a baby boy, Pratik, and was still on leave from organisational work. We had been in regular touch, and I had visited her just a few days before. All of us in JMS were shocked.

The memories of those dark days have not dimmed over the years, and I do recall how we grouped together to provide succour to each other. Prabir's strength in his hour of personal crisis and grief gave us strength, too. Indu, who had known Ashoka closely and who, in fact, became a member of the SFI through her contact with Ashoka, helped the organisation through that difficult time. I was unable to speak at Ashoka's memorial meeting. I wish I had had the strength, like Indu, to do so. I had so much to say about her: her clarity of thought, her commitment to the Party, to the movement, to socialism, her courage, her sense of fun, her ability to work hard. But I stood at the back of that packed hall, feeling like a coward, trying to hide my tears. It was difficult to bid Ashoka farewell.

We worked hard to try and fill the gap caused by Ashoka's absence. The following year, in June 1984, we held our second conference. Indu was elected president, I continued as secretary, and Kalindi became an office bearer. Fortunately for us, student activist Indrani Mazumdar became a wholetimer of the Party and said she'd like to work with JMS. She had earlier been in JNU, one of

Rita with Ashoka's son Pratik.

the youngest of her batch since she enrolled in the undergraduate languages department straight after school. She subsequently joined DU, where she led many struggles. She had also represented SFI in DVCM and the anti-dowry struggles. Her joining the JMS and taking responsibilities, including going to west Delhi and resettlement colonies, was a huge help to the organisation at a time when it was most needed. Indrani, I may add, was the daughter of Vina Mazumdar and had been a young guest at my wedding! We rebuilt our team, just as Ashoka would have liked us to do.

A 'Left' Women's Organisation

Critics of the Left often use the phrase 'party-linked organisation' derisively. They argue that when communist women build a women's organisation, it is subordinate to the dictates of the Party. We were often similarly dismissed. AIDWA had, in 1981, a membership of 12 lakh (1.2 million). The organisation had led numerous independent initiatives and struggles all over the country. All this, it appeared, amounted to nothing.

Some narratives of the course of the women's movement in the post-Emergency period have virtually photoshopped AIDWA and the Left out. In this telling, there is a presumption that communist women, or those who believe in a socialist future, have little independent agency. They act, like marionettes, at the bidding of the Party, which consists of a bunch of patriarchs. Now, one can hardly argue that each and every member or leader of the Party has been rid of patriarchal beliefs altogether. But to erase the agency of communist women within the Party does great harm to the larger cause of women's emancipation. We, communist women, have been as much part of the Party as anyone else and in my experience, we've had the space to not only speak out but actively struggle against patriarchy within and outside the Party and get the support of the Party at all levels. And this is not only true of women who come from relatively privileged middle-class backgrounds, such as myself. I have personally witnessed numerous sacrifices made and hardships faced by women from the labouring classes, from deprived and marginalised backgrounds, while working in and helping build a broad-based women's movement. They have played an extremely important and powerful role in making women's voices heard and appreciated within the Party. Women in the Party play a critical role in transforming the Party itself, in helping make the Party into a strong ally and champion of women's equality and emancipation. To write the left-oriented women's organisations like AIDWA out of the history of the women's movement is to diminish the movement itself.

For any young woman committed to fighting for women's rights, the Left and the Party provide the opportunity and the support to take that forward. Certainly, that was my and my comrades' experience in the years between 1979 and 1985 when we were building a women's organisation in Delhi.

Most of all, I cherish the memories of the dedicated, strong women activists who were such an important part of my life and many of whom continue to be so. Many of the founders of JMS became my closest friends. Kalindi was a dear friend and comrade until she died in 2009. I was inspired to see how she continued to work for the Party and AIDWA even after getting cancer. Ranjana had moved laterally to CITU in later years, working with women in the trade union movement. She died of COVID-related complications in 2020. Ashalata, another close friend and a real fighter, relocated to Hyderabad, where she continues to be active in the movement. Many working-class women I knew and became close to have either died or retired to their villages. When we occasionally get together, it is as though time rolls back, and we are back in the days of building our organisation, holding hands, returning from demonstrations, laughing at some rude comment against the police, boarding a DTC bus back to the office, loud and noisy as if to tell the world — watch out, here come the women.

V

A DECADE
CLOSES

Teachers' Struggles

In this remembering, it is convenient to sectionalise memories, but in reality, there is no such thing as 'sections' in the work that a communist does, not then as Rita and not now, decades later. When I was a child travelling on a train, I would be fascinated by the parallel tracks that seemed to merge and then separate from each other as the train sped on. In 1983, like the tracks, for me, the days merged into each other and separated, as did the different aspects of my work and responsibilities as the Party expanded into new areas.

In January 1983, the three-month historic strike of the DU teachers ended in a victory with their main demands — opening of promotion avenues and increased allowances — being conceded by the government. Veteran leaders of the teachers' movement, such as Zahoor Siddiqui, M.M.P. Singh, M.A. Javed, Ved Gupta, and Mahendra Singh, helped take the mass struggle approach forward and also helped the students' movement on the campus. M.M.P. Singh, known as Murli Babu, was one of the key leaders of the struggle, in contrast with the elected president of the Delhi University Teachers Association (DUTA), who played an extremely negative role on the issues of service conditions. He emerged as one of the most popular leaders of the teachers' movement. The secretary of the Democratic Teachers Front (DTF), which had played an important role in the struggle, was a young lecturer, P.M.S. Grewal, who drew many of his colleagues into the broader movement. Pushi, as he is affectionately called, joined the trade union movement at the end of the eighties, later resigned from his teaching job, and was elected secretary of the Delhi Party. Many young teachers in that struggle were influenced by the left-wing leadership of DUTA. I met many of these comrades in the Delhi Party office at 14 Vithalbhai Patel House on Rafi Marg and roped in Mahendra, Ved, and Zahoor to take classes in north Delhi for our Party cadre. Such advances on university campuses for Left politics provide impetus and create enthusiasm in the Party as a whole.

The 1983 Elections

In February 1983, municipal corporation and metropolitan council elections were declared in Delhi. Prakash, who had left the SFI in 1979, was working wholetime in Delhi. He was elected secretary of the Delhi Party after Major's death. He worked hard to create a non-BJP, anti-Congress electoral alliance. The Janata Party, however, decided to fight alone. Apart from CPI and other Left parties, four other parties joined us. Within the alliance, we fought five seats in the corporation and one in the council. Two of the five corporation seats were in north Delhi — Manakpura contested by Nathu Parshad and Wazirpur (which included Sawan Park), where the candidate was our handloom workers' leader, Sarwan Kumar. The Party also contested in Nand Nagri (under the Usmanpur seat), where we put up a DCM worker, Ram Niwas. I had to shuttle between these three seats.

I stayed in Nand Nagri for ten days during the elections, as too much time would have been wasted in travelling, the only mode of travel possible for me being a DTC bus. I stayed at the home of a Birla Mills worker, Mamchand, who sportingly shifted his cot outside at night while I shared the room with his wife. Ram Niwas was a reluctant candidate. We persuaded him to take leave from the mill, but it was a struggle to get him into the swing of the campaign. He disliked folding his hands and asking for votes. He would stride along beside me and when prodded, would, at best, lift a closed fist in a red salute. Since most of his voters had no idea that this was a comradely greeting, they would look at us, perplexed — *what is this*! We were low on funds, and our entire campaign was run on the generosity of textile workers living in the area, who would feed us and provide places for the volunteers to stay. On election day,

175

other political parties had put up elaborate tents near the polling booths for their volunteers. We had no money for this. So, we created our own 'booth office'. We brought out charpais — cots used by workers — tied four sticks to the corners of the wooden frame, hoisted a bed sheet on top, and decorated it with strings of red paper flags. Voila! We had a space for voters to check their names on the electoral list on their way to the booth. We got over 2,000 votes, which was not bad at all.

In Manakpura, we came close to winning. Nathu was a popular leader and energetic campaigner. A large group of young people came out in his support. His constituency included a fair number of voters from the DCM mills. They traditionally supported the Congress, but a section supported Nathu this time. On the day of the counting, we had requested a lawyer comrade, Som Dutt Sharma, to accompany our team because we apprehended that the Congress candidate would manipulate the counting of votes in his favour. We were hoping for victory, but we lost by just under 400 votes. A student from JNU, Jayaprakash N.D., who had come all the way from the campus to join the process, was quite agitated and repeatedly argued that we should be more aggressive at the counting centre. Som assessed that we did not have a strong enough case to appeal against the verdict. The young activists were devastated, and many were in tears. Nathu hid his disappointment well and cheered up his supporters with a rousing speech atop a makeshift podium, vowing to take the struggle for people's rights forward. I was proud of him. We could not match the money spent on elections by other parties. It was difficult for a party like ours, with very limited funds and with candidates who were themselves workers with low assets, to compete with wealthy opponents. Also, we found cash being given to so-called leaders in every lane, to ensure votes in their area. Liquor was also distributed generously. Our comrades were firm in their rejection of such practices.

I had a somewhat similar experience in Faridabad in 1987 when our candidate, trade union leader Mohan Lal, was contesting

Nathu Parshad campaigning during the 1983 election, which he lost by less than 400 votes.

an assembly election. He, too, preferred the closed fist as a greeting, but when gently prodded, he was more amenable than Ram Niwas to fold his hands! Mohan Lal lost the election, even though he polled a substantial number of votes among workers in his constituency. He used to be a factory worker as a young man but was dismissed for his union work. He went on to become one of the most respected trade union and Party leaders in Faridabad and Delhi. Politically sharp, a good organiser with an infectious smile, he was also highly regarded by other unions, whom he interacted with as president of Delhi CITU. We lost him to cancer in 2013.

Generally, election campaigns are extremely hard work, organisationally. The very first election campaign I had worked in was in the north Calcutta constituency of Vidyasagar in the 1971 state assembly elections in West Bengal. I worked as a volunteer under the guidance of trade union leader Shibani Sengupta, and my job was to accompany her in a house-to-house campaign. I was one of hundreds of such volunteers, each with their duty defined in a systematic and well-run campaign. Delhi and Faridabad, on the other hand, we had to depend on much smaller teams. We could not cover even half the booths. We knew we would lose, yet there was a determination to take the message of the red flag to a wider audience of voters. Some people get disheartened because they know we will not win. Other parties have money and other resources that are often literally hundreds of times what we can mobilise. Today, the decks are stacked even more heavily against parties of the working class. Bourgeois parties and their candidates spend tens of crores of rupees on assembly seats (and more on Lok Sabha seats). The opaque system of electoral bonds introduced by the BJP to conceal its close links with the corporate world and their huge donations to the party's election campaigns has further subverted the electoral process and skewed it in favour of the ruling party. The arena of electoral politics is becoming increasingly difficult for parties like the communist party, whose only asset is hard work.

Learning from Struggles

The 1983 elections had another dimension for textile workers. A month earlier, in December 1982, textile mills had gone on a one-day strike in support of Birla Mills workers. The management had shut down sections of the weaving department and threatened to retrench 3,000 permanent and badli workers. They had not been paid for eight months. While CITU and the Textile Mazdoor Congress led by Lalit Maken agreed on continuing the strike in Birla Mills if the management did not agree to halt retrenchment, the other trade unions accepted retrenchment provided the workers got some compensation. Taking advantage of the differences among the unions, the management declared a lockout. There were large gate meetings, but the management refused to budge.

One of the CITU leaders associated with the textile workers was Suraj Bhan Bhardwaj. He was a veteran trade unionist from Uttar Pradesh who had been working in the Ghaziabad region. (In our work in the Party, Ghaziabad, though in UP, is part of the Delhi state.) Bhardwaj was a well-respected and recognised trade union leader in the region. We worked closely together in the period when the union was being disrupted. Following the disruption in the union a few years earlier, his presence, along with regular consultations with national-level CITU leader M.K. Pandhe, certainly helped us, and many workers returned to the union during that struggle. Members of parliament belonging to the CPI(M) raised the issue of the lockout in parliament. Nothing worked. It was only the realisation after the local body elections were announced that since textile workers and their families were spread across many constituencies, it could hurt the ruling party electorally, they got the management to lift the lockout. It brought

Rita with Suraj Bhan Bhardwaj.

some relief to the workers. However, the basic issues remained.

In March 1983, the Birla Mills workers went on strike because the issues of retrenchment remained unsolved. It lasted over two months. We organised solidarity marches. Ashalata, who was now the main organiser of the JMS in north Delhi, took the initiative and mobilised over 500 women from textile workers' families in a solidarity march outside the central labour ministry where women courted arrest. The SFI, with Subodh as state secretary, also organised solidarity actions. Finally, the management signed an agreement that protected the workers' jobs. Retrenchment was halted. The badli workers, who were not getting any money, were paid wages for 11 days a month pending the report of a committee set up to inquire into the workers' complaints.

The political bargaining power of workers can only be felt when they move as a class united against exploitation. Bourgeois politics tries hard to break this class unity. Their trade unions play the Trojan horse within workers' struggles, as I witnessed in the textile workers' struggles. Today in India, the BJP is aggressively building an overarching majoritarian Hindutva identity based on sectarian interpretations of religion as an instrument to break workers' unity and to blunt the edge of class struggle. No divisive trick is beyond the pale for them when it comes to protecting capitalists' profits and pushing their own agenda of a Hindutva rashtra. Nothing that I experienced can compare to what the BJP is doing today to disrupt the unity of the working classes. Therefore, it is all the more essential for Left forces working among the labouring classes in India to wage the ideological battle against what the BJP is building — a pro-corporate Hindutva regime.

It was in 1983, too, that I learnt the importance of surveys and data-based analyses to build struggles and formulate demands. In September of that year, the Party's Delhi State Committee decided to conduct detailed surveys of the living conditions of residents of the resettlement colonies of Delhi. There were 18 such sprawling settlements, and we surveyed eight or nine of them. I was part of the team in Jahangirpuri and in Nand Nagri. Many students and teachers helped with the surveys. The questionnaire had been prepared by Prakash and a team at the Delhi state centre of the party. The survey was an eye-opener. The data we gathered — for example, the number of hours a woman had to spend at a water pump because most of the pumps in the area were not functional; the distance a child had to cover to reach school and the expenses involved; the lack of sanitation in the clogged public toilets; the number of people ill in a household in the previous month — drew a horrendously vivid picture of the living conditions of the urban poor in the capital city of India.

We organised a series of campaigns based on the findings of the survey. Often, our struggles are based on impressionistic or superficial readings of problems that people face. Data-based study of concrete real conditions is so much more effective. Of course, later, this became quite fashionable in NGO circles, with UN funds available for 'research-based action'. The aim there was quite different from ours. I gathered from friends involved in such surveys that the World Bank's idea was to fund projects based on surveys according to the World Bank formulae. But I did learn the importance of such work and the need to involve young, educated people in it. When I became the all-India general secretary of AIDWA a decade later, I tried to introduce the practice of survey-based mass work (among women) in the organisation.

The Build-Up to 1984

The violence and hatred against Sikhs that gripped Delhi after Indira Gandhi's assassination in 1984 was shocking and deeply distressing. I was shaken to the core, as were many of my comrades. We had sensed the deep polarisation that was developing, but the extent of the violence was as if we had been hit by a gigantic wave.

From the early eighties, there were regular reports of the growth of extremist elements with foreign support, mobilising in the name of a separate Sikh state, which developed into the movement for Khalistan. The Party in Punjab, along with the CPI, was politically fighting this trend, and our comrades were often targeted by the extremists. Under the leadership of the veteran communist leader and Polit Bureau member Harkishan Singh Surjeet, who was a member of the Rajya Sabha at the time, every forum was used by the Party to highlight the seriousness of the developing situation in Punjab. In particular, the Party warned against the politically questionable role of the Congress party and its government towards the separatist leaders. The Congress was attempting to use these elements in the fight against the main political force in Punjab, the Shiromani Akali Dal. Comrade Surjeet and the Party argued for the need to find political solutions to some of the genuine demands of the people linked to the autonomy of the state, the status of Chandigarh, the border disputes with neighbouring states, and the sharing of river waters. We stressed the importance of politically isolating the extremists instead of only resorting to repressive actions by security forces.

A look at the numerous interventions made by Comrade Surjeet on the ground — in mobilisations by the Party in Punjab; the numerous peace and harmony marches he participated in organised by the CPI(M) and the CPI; through his speeches in parliament; through his meetings with other opposition parties; his detailed memorandums submitted to the government with concrete proposals — demonstrate his prescience in understanding that India was heading towards a catastrophe. He was sharply critical of the role of the US administration and pointed out how, in Canada, too many extremist leaders found shelter and support. He warned of the dangers of communal polarisation and of the deliberate whipping up of communal sentiments by an RSS-backed platform called Hindu Suraksha Samiti.

According to official figures, between August 1982 and June 1984, when Operation Blue Star was launched, there were 1,200 violent incidents, in which 410 people were killed and 1,180 injured. Many of those killed were personnel of the security forces, but there were also targeted killings of innocent Hindus by Sikh extremists. The BJP added fuel to the fire. They called for two protest bandhs in 1984 in the neighbouring states of Rajasthan, Haryana, and Delhi. In February in Haryana, the Hindu communal forces whipped up a frenzy against the Sikh community, and there were incidents of violence in which eight Sikhs were killed, property was burnt, and Gurdwaras were attacked. It was a portent of things to come.

From January 1984 onwards, in our committee meetings at various levels, reports were coming in of the increase in anti-Sikh feelings in Delhi fuelled by the propaganda of the Hindu communalists. We held a series of public meetings following the incidents in Haryana. JMS organised a campaign in which women spoke of their fears, of the undercurrent of feeling against Sikhs in different areas. In the preparations for the second conference of JMS in June 1984, in all unit and local conferences, the urgent need for communal harmony was stressed. We explained why the Sikh extremist slogans went against the interests of working and poor people and how the Hindu communal forces were trying to take advantage of the violence in Punjab for their own gains. Women reported the wild rumours which were rife in many areas — such as how the Sikhs were poisoning all water sources in colonies or that there were gangs waiting outside schools to kidnap children. Clearly, organised communal forces were at work.

Anti-communal Organising

In May 1984, the Party held a week-long campaign in Delhi for communal harmony. We distributed thousands of leaflets door-to-door throughout Delhi. In north Delhi, on the main roads leading up to DCM, there were several tyre shops owned by Sikhs. One day, I was accompanying our team in the leafletting campaign. We were invited into one of the shops by an elderly Sikh. He spoke in a whisper and told us that after the Haryana incidents, they did not feel safe. In Roshanara Bagh, too, where Chenni and her family lived, we held small meetings, urging the residents not to pay heed to communal slogans. Many of those whom we had contacted in the campaign joined the Party's dharna on 21 May outside the PM's residence, demanding a political intervention.

As part of this campaign, Janam produced a play written by Safdar called *Veer Jag Zara* (*Arise Oh Brave One!*), where the protagonist was the state of Punjab. Some of the dialogue was in Punjabi, and Safdar was quite pleased as it was his first attempt at writing in Punjabi! There were many songs in the play, too, and in some of the shows, the main actor's role was performed by Madan Gopal Singh, whose mellifluous singing mesmerised the crowds. Many were moved to tears when they watched the performance. It was an effective play in which the separatists, as well as those promoting communal divisions, were exposed. Unfortunately, the play's run was cut short when Operation Blue Star took place in June, and the entire situation changed dramatically.

We had a discussion in our Party Local committee. My effort was to ensure at least that our own members and sympathisers were free from the communal virus spreading rapidly through the city and that they became active participants in their own areas to spread the message of harmony. The situation worsened after the army stormed the Golden Temple and killed Bhindranwale and his armed supporters. While the army's action on the revered gurdwara distressed Sikhs and others, the discovery of a huge cache of arms, newly-built tunnels and bunkers, and detailed military-style planning by the extremists showed that they had no concern for maintaining the sanctity of the temple either. The deep hurt to the psyche of the community due to the storming of the sanctum sanctorum by the army and the consequent destruction overwhelmed everything else. In September, there was another horrendous incident. A large number of Hindus, including women and children, were pulled out of a bus in Gurdaspur and shot dead by extremists in retribution for Operation Blue Star. The tremors were felt in Delhi. The BJP and the RSS along with many who belonged to the Congress party, started organising marches in different areas with provocative slogans.

We held neighbourhood meetings in industrial areas and gate meetings at the mills on these issues. There was a muted response. While people wanted to know the position of CITU and the Party, there wasn't any great enthusiasm. The number of Sikh workers in the mills was negligible. In the industrial areas, the numbers were greater, and many were members of the CITU. But it was clear that workers, too, were getting infected with the communal propaganda. This was the situation in Delhi on the eve of Indira Gandhi's cold-blooded assassination by her two Sikh bodyguards.

That morning of 31 October, I was at my eye doctor's. Dr Malik's clinic was in a lane off Connaught Place. I had developed painful lesions in my eyes over the previous several months. It was so bad that I had to have one eye bandaged for over a week. Dr Malik had just finished prescribing the eye drops I had to use, when his assistant came running into his chamber with the shocking news that Indira Gandhi had been shot. Dr Malik switched on the radio. There was no television in his chamber. We heard the news, numbly. I got into an auto rickshaw and went straight back to Vitthalbhai Patel House. Prakash had already left with our parliamentary group leader Samar Mukherjee for AIIMS, where Mrs Gandhi had been taken. I stayed at the Party office, constantly in touch with our units in north Delhi and with JMS.

By evening, we started hearing news of sporadic incidents of violence against Sikhs. From the night of 31 October to 3 November, widespread violence engulfed Delhi. Sikhs were attacked, lynched, burnt, murdered, and their businesses and homes looted and gutted. It was horrific.

I got a call from Manakpura that attacks had started against Sikhs in the area on the morning of 1 November. Rahul Verma, Major Saheb's son, who had become a trade union activist in the industrial areas of north Delhi, was in the Party office. Although the police posted there advised us not to go out, we got onto his motorcycle and sped to Manakpura. On the way, we saw spirals of black smoke across the skies of Delhi. I will always remember the scene we encountered in the main market in Manakpura. There was Nathu Parshad, with a small group of comrades standing on the road confronting a baying crowd who wanted to burn a shop owned by a Sikh. A woman with a Congress flag was screaming at Nathu. 'My mother has been killed [she meant Indira Gandhi], step aside, we want to teach the killers a lesson', she said. She was supported by a slogan-shouting crowd. We stood with Nathu and did not budge. The crowd turned away. A little while later, Nathu was called to a meeting by local Congress leaders. They told him to stay away from the area from 2-6 pm that day so that they could avenge 'their mother's killing'. Their target were the 35 or more Sikh families living in an adjoining area called Doriwalan. For three days and nights, under Nathu's leadership, a group of communists and local residents stood guard in the area, preventing violence against Sikh families and their homes.

We went to the DCM lines where Bishen Pal and others lived. Most of the workers were in the mill. Bishen Pal was keeping watch with a group of workers. He told us that they were trying to prevent workers from joining the mobs that were looting and burning shops on the main road. Many tyre shops had been looted and burnt. It was a dreadful, horrendous scene. We went to Roshanara Bagh. There were crowds outside the road. In the colony where our office was located, young men were running from the main road to the side lanes carrying goods stolen from the shops they had broken into.

I went to the lane where Chenni lived. Many young Sikhs of the area had taken shelter there as they knew that Gyani Amar Singh had a licensed gun. He told us, 'If anyone touches even a hair on the heads of my girls, I will kill them before I die'. That night, a mob came to attack Sikh houses, including Chenni's. They were saved by the brave actions of the residents of the 'Harijan Basti', an area mainly inhabited by Dalits who came out on the road to prevent any attacks. Fortunately, the gun remained unused. For the next few days, the area was protected by the Dalits and other Hindu residents of the area. But tragedy awaited Gyani Amar Singh's family. Chenni got a message that her sister, Guggi, recently married and living in east Delhi, had been attacked, her in-laws' home burnt and that she, along with her husband, had been taken by the army to a camp in Nanaksar. Brave Chenni reached there on her own to bring her sister to safety. She found her sister in a state of terror. Guggi's brother-in-law had been caught by a mob, his hair cut, and a burning tyre put around his neck. He died of burns. Another sister, Balwinder Kaur, had a narrow escape, as she was saved by her Hindu neighbours. The neighbours cut her husband's hair to conceal his Sikh identity and hid them in their house. Despite these multiple tragedies, a few days later, Chenni was in the Jahangirpuri relief camp, working hard with our volunteers, and providing relief.

In the Wazirpur industrial area, workers came out to protect Sikh-owned factories which were targeted by the mobs. Workers of Birla Mills and ATM reported that most workers stayed inside the mills. In Sawan Park, our units mobilised and prevented outsiders from attacking a neighbouring colony which housed many Sikh families. In several places, Party units had mobilised to save Sikhs. In Vitthalbhai Patel House, comrades who were in the office, including Prakash and some young SFI boys, heard that a local taxi stand was being attacked. They rushed out and managed to save the taxi drivers, all Sikhs, and their cars. There were individual cases of bravery, too, like that of Vandana, a comrade working at the party centre, who was travelling in an auto rickshaw with her small child when she saw a young Sikh boy being attacked. She intervened, pulled him into the vehicle, and tried to hide him. But hardly had the autorickshaw moved when a crowd stopped it and demanded to search it. Vandana clutched onto the boy, fought to prevent him from being dragged away. By then, her own child was screaming in terror. The Sikh boy was taken away. She tried to find out where he was but could get no news. Even years later, when she recalls that dreadful day, tears stream down her face — 'I tried my best, but I couldn't save him'.

Similar reports were pouring in from Party units all over Delhi. Many resettlement colonies where we had units like Nand Nagri, Mangolpuri, Sultanpuri, and Jahangirpuri were badly affected, and comrades reported their despair and grief that they could do little, being overpowered by the huge numbers of rioters and killers. For three full days and nights, Delhi turned into hell, where mobs instigated by Congress leaders and Hindu communal groups conducted killings, looting, burning, and general mayhem. In all this, the police played the role of active connivers. In one of the most horrific cases of violence ever in Delhi, Block 32 of Trilokpuri in east Delhi witnessed the massacre of over 300 Sikhs. After three days of bloodletting, the death toll stood at over 2,500. It was hard even to estimate the destruction of property and livelihoods.

Relief Work After the Violence

The Party formed a relief committee with Ved Gupta as the convenor. I was a member along with Indu and representatives of other mass organisations. The government had set up makeshift camps in various places. We decided we would concentrate our efforts where we had some units in areas such as Jahangirpuri, Mangolpuri, Sultanpuri, Nand Nagri, and Shakurpur.

On 4 November, we called a meeting of the JMS committee. We got first-hand reports of the situation in various areas. We decided on three immediate steps — relief work in the camps; peace marches in residential areas; and special efforts to contact women who had been widowed and to raise their demands before the authorities.

The Delhi Party and mass organisations worked round the clock for the next few weeks. It was the first experience for most of us to directly confront the horror, sadness, and grief of communal violence and its consequences. We divided responsibilities. I was mainly stationed in Jahangirpuri, although I went to all the other camps as well to ensure relief supplies. The camp in Jahangirpuri was run by the SFI led by Subodh and JMS comrades organised by Ashalata. About 200 families had been brought by the army from surrounding areas. Among them were at least a hundred women whose husbands had been killed, often before their eyes. I remember a mother whose son was missing. She sat in front of the police station for days, pleading for help. It was heartbreaking. I don't know if that mother ever found her son.

In all the camps where we worked, we were helping families fill up the forms required for compensation, for accommodation, and for copies of their documents which had been burnt. Many cases of sexual violence were reported to us by the women. There was little hope for justice, as the perpetrators could not be identified. Kalindi had done a detailed record of women's testimonies in Nand Nagri. Although the official registration of deaths was much less, Kalindi and the team registered 125 deaths. She had met many of the widows. She had also recorded statements of sexual attacks. Based on the women's reports, some local politicians were arrested, but intervention by East Delhi member of parliament, H.K.L. Bhagat, got them released.

The impunity of the powerful was staggering. The culpability of the government, the ruling party, the communal forces, the police — nothing was secret. We organised peace marches in many areas. The campaign and meetings we had held earlier that year had, to a great extent, been instrumental in our being able to mobilise our workers for relief work and for initiatives like peace marches. We were able to inoculate our own members and followers from the virus of communal hatred, which seemed to rage through the city like a deadly pandemic.

Because of our collective initiatives, we could contact many women directly affected by the violence. On 23 November, the JMS held the first demonstration in Delhi on demands of the widowed women. Among the hundreds who participated were 120 women whose husbands were killed in the violence. It was an important intervention, and the memorandum we gave to the Lt. Governor exposed the cruel and criminal negligence of the government towards the special needs of widows. Our surveys had shown a much larger number of deaths than registered by the authorities. We highlighted the desperate need for permanent accommodation, of skill training, of jobs, of free education for children, of a monthly stipend to cover household expenses pending employment for the survivor families. We also pointed out the need for counselling and social infrastructures of support.

It was a hard lesson we all learnt. To witness at such close quarters the extent of the inhumanity that can be aroused on communal lines was staggering. To be anguished about the heinous killing of a leader, no matter how beloved, is one thing, but to use that to fuel hatred and spread poison against an entire community is altogether different. It demonstrated the fragility of the constitutional values of secularism and democracy. An encouraging fact for us in that gloom was that there was one state in India where the violence was immediately quelled even though there was a substantial Sikh population, and that was West Bengal. The Left Front government moved decisively. Chief Minister Jyoti Basu warned the would-be rioters that the police had been issued shoot-at-sight orders. But it wasn't only the government that acted out of a sense of responsibility. Hundreds of red volunteers came out on the streets of Calcutta and Asansol and other centres where Sikhs lived, working for communal harmony and assuring them of protection. We spoke about the West Bengal example in all our meetings and at peace marches in Delhi. The West Bengal example certainly inspired our comrades.

The experience brought home to us the dangers of ignoring or underestimating the power of communal forces. The role of Congress politicians and the connivance of the state, particularly the Delhi Police, with the perpetrators of violence is well documented. However, what we had found was that there was another force working to spread communal hate, and that was the RSS and its associated organisations. This was also highlighted in some of the later official inquiries. The Jain-Aggarwal Committee had examined the affidavits of many of the survivors and recommended the registration of FIRs against BJP and RSS leaders. Subsequently, 14 FIRs were lodged, which named 49 of their leaders. One of them, Ram Kumar Jain, had been the election agent of Shri Atal Bihari Vajpayee in 1980.

The Delhi Party had its conference in the following year, 1985. The State Committee, in its review of the last three years, said, 'The most important factor influencing the political life of Delhi during this period was the danger represented by the separatist and communal forces'. What we were referring to was not only the anti-Sikh propaganda and violence but also the Vishwa Hindu Parishad-led Ram Janmbhoomi agitation, which had also begun by then. In the next eight years, that agitation, which culminated in the destruction of the Babri Masjid in Ayodhya on 6 December 1992, was to leave behind a trail of blood and destruction across the country, the consequences of which we are still facing today.

Delhi Party

By 1984, I was spending more time at the Delhi Party centre and at the women's organisation centre. My interaction with comrades at the centre increased. One of the skills a leader has to have is to identify the right person for the job at hand, known in organisational terms as 'deployment of cadre'. P. Sundarayya, the first General Secretary of the Party, always stressed this requirement for the expansion of work, and it was reflected in the work of the Delhi Party leadership, too. During the brutal attacks on the party in West Bengal in the early seventies and the foisting of false cases, several comrades from West Bengal took on aliases and worked in different states, including Delhi. Here, they were deployed in different fields. Of them, three stayed on in Delhi even after the Emergency: Ajit Bhattacharya, Jayant Rai alias Sushil Bhattacharya, and Sanjay Banerjee alias Tamal Mitra. They helped the Delhi Party enormously. Sushil Bhattacharya later became Lok Sabha member from Burdwan, West Bengal, in 1980, but he continued to be associated with the Delhi Party and trade unions. Ajit Bhattacharya was a trade union leader and secretary of the party committee in south Delhi till he returned to West Bengal a few years later. Tamal was one of the founders of the Democratic Youth Federation (DYFI) in Delhi. He was a wonderful comrade, fearless, highly political, and with an ability to lead in the most challenging of situations. He lived in the small verandah attached to the Delhi Party office at V.P. House, with hardly any personal needs. I worked closely with him in north Delhi, where he helped to develop DYFI units. Tamal returned to West Bengal some years later, working in the jute workers' union.

I also got to know many other comrades working in the trade

unions in other areas and sectors. I remember the comrades in the Life Insurance Corporation (LIC), where we had a strong unit. One of their leaders, B.K. Paliwal was a fount of information on public sector units (PSU), their importance to the economy, and so on. This was well before the privatisation spree started. He would repeatedly stress that PSU unions needed to be in close touch with the people they served — insurance holders, bank account holders, and others. This was necessary, he felt, both to serve the people better and to get public support if the LIC took steps which would affect their interests. There is much propaganda by ruling circles and regimes against the 'privileged' public sector workers. Divisions are sought to be created between different sections of workers. A leader like Paliwal was sensitive to such propaganda and directly worked with the union to counter such attempts. LIC was one of the most important and politically active unions, and Paliwal tried to involve employees in campaigns outside as well.

Communist Families

At the trade union centre, the senior-most comrade — not in age, but in terms of experience — was Jogendra Sharma, who had started working for the Party in 1969 in various capacities and got his membership in 1973. After the Emergency, while Sushil Bhattacharya was general secretary, he became the secretary of Delhi CITU and subsequently secretary of the Party's south Delhi local committee after Ajit Bhattacharya returned to West Bengal. In 1985, when Prakash shifted to the all-India centre of the Party, Jogendra was elected secretary of the Delhi state committee. He quit his job and became a wholetime cadre of the party. We worked closely for many years. Among the many initiatives he took as secretary of the Delhi Party was the building of a broad-based platform for communal harmony and secularism — Committee for Communal Harmony (CCH). In the second half of 1986, he played a crucial role in building a campaign through CCH across Delhi. This culminated in one of the most well-attended marches for communal harmony in the history of Delhi. It saw participation from a wide cross-section of people — school teachers and students; intellectuals, artists, journalists, lawyers, and other professionals; and thousands of workers and employees from several trade unions and mass organisations.

Another comrade I worked closely with was Sohail Hashmi. He was a student at JNU but had left his PhD halfway (and the scholarship that went with it) to work wholetime for the party. He was a key functionary of the students' organisation, and later took up responsibilities in the youth organisation with Tamal and others.

For communists, it is a matter of pride if we belong to a

communist family or if we can persuade others in our family to join the Party or to work as sympathisers. When leaders like Narendra Modi talk contemptuously of politics based on family connections, we need to remind them that they are talking of their own kind from parties representing the ruling classes. In our movement, being part of a communist family means sacrifice, deprivation, and more sacrifice. Even though we were a small force in Delhi, we did have quite a few examples. There were so many couples among our working-class comrades who worked for the Party. In north Delhi there were Sarwan Kumar and his wife Prasanni; Dayanand and Gita; Inder Pal and Kamla; Yashpal and Kamla, and decades later, their two daughters; and many more. The reason I mention this is because in a city like Delhi, the communist party is weak, and being a member affords no hope of any benefits. On the contrary, you risk losing your job or your livelihood. Despite this, so many comrades involved their family members.

Among middle-class families, too, there were such examples. Both Jogendra and Sohail, with different personal histories, had one thing in common — a communist family. Sohail's mother, Qamar Azad, was a much-loved schoolteacher who spent her free time organising women in JMS at the time of its foundation. Sohail's sister Shehla was active in Janam for a while and is married to P.M.S. Grewal ('Pushi'), former secretary of the Delhi Party. Another sister, Shabnam, is also involved with many movements. Sohail's younger brother was the brilliant and charismatic artist Safdar Hashmi, who married Moloyashree, a communist. Her parents, the trade unionist J.C. Roy and JMS member Aparna Roy, were also staunch Party members. Jogendra's partner Kiran worked in the Party's Hindi publication *Lok Lahar* and was an early activist of the JMS. She was the office secretary for the Delhi Party. His siblings — Vijendra, a front-ranking leader of the teachers' movement and of the Delhi Party, a much-beloved comrade who passed too early, as well as Veena, Renu, and Devendra — were all active in the Party. Then there are the Mazumdar siblings, children of the redoubtable Vina Mazumdar — Shashwati, a prominent leader of the teachers' movement; Indrani, who started as a student activist and then became a wholetimer and leader of JMS; Ranjani, a former students' movement activist and co-founder of Delhi's first women's film making collective Mediastorm; and Surajit, a former president of the JNU Students' Union and now a teachers' movement leader, who is married to the journalist T.K. Rajalakshmi, who has consistently brought to light stories of women and workers. There are so many other such examples.

Being a Woman in the Party

In the decade that I cover in this book, there were around a thousand or so members of the Party in Delhi. We worked together and knew each other well, but it was not as though there were no differences or tensions between us. In my Rita years, I used to make New Year's resolutions. I still do. As Rita, my resolve would usually be to address differences and tensions in a better way, such as, 'Count to ten before reacting in a disagreement during a meeting' or 'Control expressions and body language in responses'. I was impetuous in those days, though my work in the trade unions did temper that down substantially.

Between 1982 and 1985, Prakash was the Secretary of the Party in Delhi. When I look back, I can appreciate the culture prevalent in the Party in Delhi in those days. I never felt that I was being judged or that my work or opinions were linked to my relationship with Prakash. I was independent and free to express my views without bothering about anything else. Of course, it helped that my sphere of work was entirely different or independent of that of Prakash's, whether in the trade union, as a secretary of a local committee or in the women's organisation. It is true, though, that as a woman, to get one's work recognised does take more effort.

The reason for my appreciation of the Delhi experience is because, as I learnt, it is not always that way. In my later life, when I was taking up more responsibilities in the Party and in other organisations beyond Delhi, at the national level, I found that often my own identity as a communist, as a woman, as a wholetimer of the Party for so many decades, was all conflated with my being Prakash's wife. At a time of political differences, of which there were quite a few occasions, this gets exacerbated, driven also by motivated gossip in the media. Whatever the reason, I became more aware or rather I was forced to be more self-conscious of my relations with comrades. I had to deal with the burden of additional scrutiny. I did learn to do so, though sometimes, snide comments published in the press were an irritant.

It is the collective efforts of an increasing number of women in the Party, strong, independent, making their opinions and voices heard, who have made the radical difference in developing an independent identity of women communists. When a young woman joining the Party sometimes asks me for advice on her personal life, this is what I say: if you do want to marry, choose someone who has the same ideological and political views as your own — but right from the start strike an independent path — and never ever sacrifice your own views, never succumb to pressure. If you reach a responsible position in the Party, always look out for those who may face patriarchal hurdles or barriers. Help make the path easier for those who will come after you.

As Rita, I never really had to face these problems, which is why I can better appreciate the comrades with whom I had worked with in Delhi all those decades ago.

My Rita Decade

In 1985, I was relieved of my responsibility as secretary of the Party's north Delhi committee. It was ten years since I had begun working in north Delhi as Rita. I had mixed feelings as I left. At one level, I was excited to be taking on other responsibilities, particularly since my involvement on women's issues became an important part of my thinking, and I wanted to devote more time to such work. But equally, I was sad to be giving up my daily interactions with comrades whom I had worked with so closely for a decade. Kamal Narayan took over my responsibility as secretary. He and I had shared many experiences and ups and downs together, particularly when we were dealing with disruptions in the textile workers' union. In his speech, as he took over charge from me, he said, 'Rita can never escape from us, because even in her dreams, the mill gate siren will always sound loud and clear'. In the decades that have followed, my responsibilities in the movement have taken me in different directions, but it is true that the sound of the siren, calling workers to join the shift, has remained as a metaphor for all that I have learnt, as well as a call to action.

My education as Rita at the mill gates in Delhi, at the homes of the workers, the experiences of working in urban bastis, the experience of working at the local level as secretary of a committee, the excitement of collective involvement in the building of a women's organisation, learning how to be a partisan in the fight against exploitation, however adverse the conditions, enjoying the love, the fun, the shared moments of life, the lows and the highs with those one calls comrades — provided an anchor for me in the sometimes stormy days ahead.

Postscript

As part of the research for this memoir, I was reading through the minutes of meetings of the Delhi State Committee of the Party. My signature as being present in the meeting held on 11 November 1985 was as Rita; a month later, on 17 December, I signed the minutes as Brinda. A chapter — stretching across ten years — in my life had ended.

Rita getting arrested, Delhi, mid-1980s.

Acknowledgements

In the first half of 2022, I got a call from my niece and Marxist author, Elisabeth Armstrong, who lives and teaches in the US. She evinced a keen interest in learning about my experiences as a young woman working in a male-dominated trade union, and that too during the Emergency. Over several hours of telephonic conversations, interrupted by our busy schedules, I relived those days through the many questions she asked. When I forgot dates, it was Elizabeth who dug out published reports of a strike or a demonstration to jog my memory. Thank you, Lisa.

I also thank my friend and colleague Indu Agnihotri. Coincidentally, it was around the same time that Indu urged me to write about our experiences in the early days of the formation of a left-oriented women's organisation in Delhi. 'You better write it out now, before we start forgetting.' She made many suggestions for the section on the JMS, for which I am grateful.

This led me to search for documents. I found a wealth of detail in the records of the meetings of the Delhi State Committee of the CPI(M) and those of the JMS. I thank the comrades who helped me access these documents.

Unfortunately, the records of the Kapda Mazdoor Lal Jhanda Union were ruined when the trunk they were stored in got submerged during a particularly heavy monsoon when rainwater flooded the union office. In the absence of written records, I had to rely solely on the memories of the former unionists who live in Delhi. I thank Bishen Pal, Chhote Lal, Dayanand, Harish Chander Pant, Nathu Parshad, Ram Pal, Shiv Kumar, and Sohan Lal for the time and memories they shared with me. I am grateful to my comrade, Pushpinder Grewal, who did a fact-check through all the different versions of the manuscript.

I would like to thank my sister Radhika for her insightful suggestions and my nieces Atiya and especially Mandakini for their comments on an early version. I also thank my cousin from Jhamapukur, Bhatindra Nath Mitra, for details of the Mitra family tree.

Writing a memoir while constantly on the move, in between meetings, demonstrations, and travel, seemed impossible. After I had written the first chapter, I was ready to give up. I sent it to Vijay Prashad, my brilliant nephew and Editor at LeftWord Books. Within a day, I got an encouraging response, and I thought I should soldier on. Vijay is responsible for my not abandoning this book mid-way.

My special thanks and regards are for Sudhanva Deshpande, Managing Editor at LeftWord Books and the main editor of this book. He really helped put the narrative in this book in shape. We had a lot of back and forth. It was he who persuaded me to add some more personal details, which I had wanted to avoid. But for him and Vijay, this memoir would never have been completed. I am fortunate to have had them as my editors.

I have very few photos of my Rita decade. I thank my comrades and friends who shared the photos reproduced in this book. A special thanks to Jana Natya Manch for letting me use photos (pp. 84, 121, 147) from their archive.

None of the people I've thanked are in any way responsible for the omissions and commissions in this book, for which I am solely responsible.

Some people said to me that a memoir should be of a life, not merely of a decade. Several comrades felt that it was unusual for a memoir to be only about ten years out of the over fifty years of my public life. Well, frankly, that's all I could manage. I write about a different time. Looking back, the Emergency seems like a short nightmare. It was over before two years had passed. How relieved we were. But today, under the present regime, we seem to be living in a constant state of siege, not knowing which pillar of our secular democratic republic will be bulldozed next. It is a time to act, for each one of us to stand up and be counted, no matter where we are and what we do.

More strength to our struggle to save India, to save democracy and secularism, to save the Constitution. More strength to our battle against class exploitation, gender oppression, and for the elimination of caste.